SHANIKO
From Wool Capital to Ghost Town

Cover photo: Shaniko Hotel appears much as it did in 1901 when Fen Batty opened its doors to business under the name of Columbia Southern Hotel. Kelly Schneider added life to the scene as she drove her miniature horse, Rusty Fire, and cart up the street of the Ghost Town of Shaniko.

SHANIKO · OREGON IN 1910

Looking north on L Street, Hotel Shaniko on the right, Eagle Hotel is in the left foreground, Columbia Southern Hotel in far center.

SHANIKO

From Wool Capital to Ghost Town

By
Helen Guyton Rees

Binford & Mort Publishing
Portland, Oregon

DEDICATED
to
Bill and Lillie Rees

SHANIKO
From Wool Capital to Ghost Town

Printed in the United States of America

Library of Congress Catalog Card Number: 81-70285

ISBN 0-8323-0538-3

First Edition 1982
Second Edition 1990
Third Edition 2002

APPRECIATION

Among our dear friends, the Rev. and Mrs. Dick Morgan have been foremost in encouraging me to write down memories of pioneer life in Oregon. Dick Morgan passed along an electric typewriter to make it easier. Since I began compiling Shaniko history, Mary Morgan has been a constant source of encouragement, spending countless hours as advisor and critic.

Doris Sias has been another staunch supporter. From the time I began writing "Schoolmarms," the story of my mother's teaching experiences at Bakeoven, Doris has continued to give me ideas, tips, and "how-to" books. Our niece, Rena Peterson, typed some of the first draft of that manuscript, getting me off to a good start.

Mary Ada "Pat" Rose, who grew up in Shaniko and lived there after we left, has carefully copied photos and familiar scenes and kept us up to date on events since 1942.

Particular thanks go to Col. Lewis Nichols, Jim Weeks, Fritz Cramer, Jean Krier and Gladys Seufert, who have read the manuscript and commented. Their evaluation and advice are truly appreciated. Many thanks also goes to Harry Hill for his first-hand account of early goings-on in Shaniko.

I count as good friends the people who have trusted me with their pictures, family stories, and anecdotes of Shaniko days, and the many people who have written me concerning some phase of the work. Thank you:

C. W. Altermatt, Bertha Berg, Lottie Borthwick, Alida Brown, Madge Brown, Mr. & Mrs. Leo Butcher, Pink Butler, Mr. & Mrs. Clarence Ellis, Amos Fine, Mr. & Mrs.

Dave Gastman, Gayle Hahn, Celia Hays, Agnes Hinkle, Bob Hinton, Clarence Hunt, Elman Jones, Mr. & Mrs. Tommy Jones, John Joyce, Margaret Kimsey, Ethel Kinney, Elinor Kiskila, Ernest Kramer, Ed Martin, Helen McMennamin, Ivan Olsen, Ernest Patjens.

Lulu Paullus, the Rev. Louis Perkins, John Reeder, Ralph Reeder, Adelbert Rees, Harry Rees, Jim Rees, Jack Rees, Alice Roberts, Pat Rose, Frances Schilling, Chatty Silvertooth, Sonny Spalinger, Elizabeth Spires, Glade and Vergil Steinmetz, Lois Steward, Paul & Thelma Stoutt, Mr. & Mrs. Frank Wagner, Julia Wakerlig, George Ward, Eugene Werner, Sue Widmark, Cora Willich, Van Woodside.

H.G.R.

CONTENTS

FOREWORD

For more than forty years visitors have gone to the Ghost Town of Shaniko to renew memories or capture in imagination a glimpse of the "Wool Capital of the World" as it was in 1901–1911. Unfortunately, feature stories that appeared in magazines and newspapers were based more on fiction than fact. It seemed that the writers relied on exaggerated tales, misinformation, and western lore, to describe a pioneer city with some sophistication.

Someone was needed to set the record straight regarding the events that followed the coming of the railroad to its terminal on the high desert of Central Oregon. When I became interested in genealogy I began to write our family histories, and found there a record unfolding of life in the early days of Shaniko. From the beginning, members of our families had lived in Shaniko. Bill and Lillie Rees, my husband's parents, married, raised their family, and lived out their lives there. Bill owned all the warehouses for many years. The warehouse record boos were available to me, as were the City Council Proceedings.

My father, Will Guyton, was a cowboy in the area before the trains came in 1901. My mother, Ada Bell, had kept a diary of her school-teaching days at nearby Bakeoven in 1897. Glade Steinmetz, their first daughter, was in business for forty years in Shaniko. My husband, Adelbert Rees was raised, and we spent the first thirteen years of our married life there!

Our families are keepers of memorabilia and friendships. We know, personally, most of the people who lived for any length of time in the "Wool Capital." It became inevitable that I should write the history of Shaniko.

With more naievete' than skill I began gathering material for the history in 1976. In the ensuing years some evidence of the undertaking has always been visible in boxes of papers, letters, or records accumulating in our kitchen, for the research necessary to make the account historically accurate.

If this history dispels some of the myths and allows the personalities of the early residents to be understood in the pioneering and homesteading context of their day, I will be glad. In addition to that, if it enables the reader to understand the importance of the city in *its* generation—that will be good. And if it helps other generations to appreciate the rigors and struggles of pioneering, homesteading, ranching and home-making in an undeveloped land, this book will have achieved its purpose.

1

IN THE BEGINNING

In 1860, the high desert of southern Wasco County was a vast, silent land of bunchgrass dotted with sagebrush and rock scabs, all encompassed by the blue dome of sky and ringed about with distant purple hills.

During the first three years of the 20th century, this lonely plateau was transformed into the "Wool Capital of the World." The City of Shaniko fairly leaped into being when the Columbia Southern Railroad Company terminated its line at Cross Hollows in 1900.

For the following 10 years, Shaniko was the hub of transportation and the business center for the wool, wheat, cattle, and sheep raised on 20,000 square miles of Oregon's interior. There was no other such center east of the Cascade mountains, even into Idaho and south to Klamath Falls and beyond with rail connections to the main line. When there was a wool sale, millions of dollars changed hands in a day. People came in to take up homestead land; they flocked to the rail terminal to travel north, south, east and west. They hurried to Shaniko to buy ranch supplies, to transact business, and to refresh themselves at the several saloons.

The name "Shaniko" is unique. No other place in the world bears this name, for it is an original simplification of the German name, Scherneckau.

The story of Shaniko begins with the discovery of gold at Canyon City in 1862. Thousands of miners were pushing into Oregon's High Country to reach this canyon located 190 or so miles from the early settlement at The Dalles. Reaching the interior of Oregon was difficult even on horseback. There were no roads, so pack trains carried supplies. Miners walked, or rented horses to ride.

The route taken to Canyon City extended south from The Dalles, crossing the Deschutes River, then continuing southeast with camps located where water was found. Two of these camps east of the Deschutes River are of particular interest, bearing on the history of Shaniko. The first, now known as Bakeoven, became a farming community closely associated with Shaniko. The second stop was eight miles over the sagebrush and bunchgrass-tufted hill in the crossing of two hollows where several springs were found. The place became known as Cross Hollows. It is located in a draw within the present city limits of Shaniko, but it was to be 38 years before that city came into being.

In the 1860's transporting gold was a risky business. Hostile Indians and the fear of robbery brought complaints that finally reached Washington, D.C. In February 1867, the State of Oregon received a grant for the contruction of a military wagon road from The Dalles to Fort Boise, Idaho. A road of sorts was built.

During the years of traffic between The Dalles and Canyon City, homesteaders began appearing in Central Oregon.

By the time the gold diggings at Canyon City had run out and the traffic had dwindled away, much of the best land around Cross Hollows and Bakeoven had been claimed. Credit for the rapid development of commerce, when the railroad was built, must go to the homesteaders, sheep-men, and ranchers who had settled in Central Oregon by 1898.

There was a period between the rush for gold and the rush to the rail line when pioneering was a lonely way of life. Some of the people who had raised sheep on the bleak hills around Cross Hollows were glad to find land in more sheltered canyons around Bakeoven. To tell the story of Cross Hollows during these interim years, is also to tell the story of Bakeoven, for it was pretty much one area.

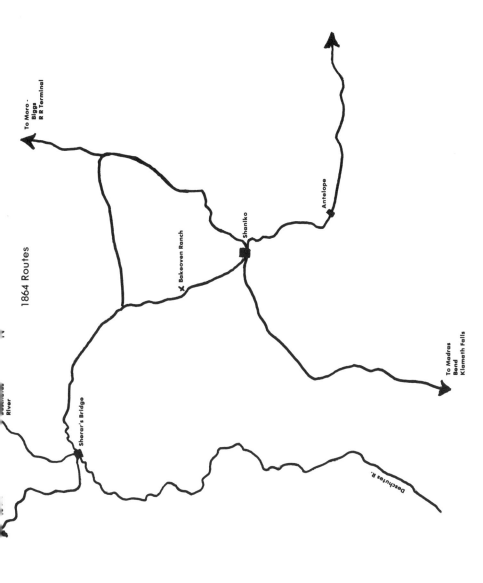

Map of the early routes to the gold fields in 1864. What is now Shaniko was at a cross-road between the north-south route from the Columbia River to the California gold fields and the route being taken east-west from The Dalles to the Canyon City diggings.

Central Oregon Stages
in
Cow Canyon

Roads were practically non-existent.

Hauling freight by ox-team before roads had been built.

The first owners of the land around Cross Hollows were John and Elizabeth Ward, who bought 160 acres of land from The Dalles Military Road Co. Thomas Ward, a stage driver from The Dalles, built the first inn and blacksmith shop. It is not known if the two Wards were related. From 1864 until 1874, Thomas Ward provided food, lodging, and road services to miners and suppliers on their way to Canyon City.

August Scherneckau

August Scherneckau, for whom the City of Shaniko is named, and his wife, Cicilia, came to Cross Hollows in 1874. Scherneckau and his partner Richard Closter (about whom little is known) bought the holdings of Thomas H. Ward. About five years later, Closter sold his share to Scherneckau and left. As the business expanded, Scherneckau built a store, a saloon, and eventually, a 16-room inn. It was not long until he was doing a $50,000-a-year business. He bought more land, invested in sheep, and hired some of the immigrant newcomers as herders.

In May 1879, Scherneckau opened a post office and became the first postmaster. In May 1884, Charles W. Haight became the second postmaster, but only until August of that year, when Mr. Scherneckau again took it over. In December of 1887 Gustav Schmidt became the fourth and last postmaster at Cross Hollows.

Mr. Farr was bookkeeper for Scherneckau during these prosperous years. When the gold rush to Canyon City had slacked off, Mr. Scherneckau sold his business to Mr. Farr and moved to Astoria, Oregon.

August Scherneckau was a native of Rensburg, Schleswig-Holstein who came to New York in March 1858, then went to Davenport, Iowa. A year later he accompanied other German immigrants to Nebraska. In 1860, a prairie fire burned out most of the community, including provisions, and nearly starved the settlers. They weathered the year, and in 1861 Scherneckau regarded himself as having reached his ideal - a cabin measuring 12 x 16 feet, and 160 acres of land he could call his own.

Thereafter, he spent three years as a soldier in the Civil War, until he was wounded in the knee and went home for a period to recover. While recuperating, he found he could ride a horse, so he joined his reorganized regiment to fight the Plains Indians, at that time menacing the settlers.

Eventually he became discouraged, because of the lack of fuel and building materials in Nebraska, and decided to seek a home where timber was more plentiful; but first, he returned to Germany to visit. When he left his fatherland, he was accompanied by his bride, Miss Cicilia Miller. They lived in Grand Island, Nebraska for a while, but in 1869 they turned their faces west and joined an ox-drawn caravan of wagons with the destination of Cheyenne, Wyoming. Not yet satisfied, they continued their westward trek and in 1874 they arrived at Cross Hollows, Wasco County, Oregon. For 10 years the Scherneckaus were content to develop the business at Cross Hollows, before selling out and leaving for Astoria, Oregon where Mrs. Scherneckau died.

Mr. Scherneckau decided to return to Germany for a visit. The outbreak of the First World War caught him still there, and he remained for the duration of the war. Though he had taken out his United States Citizenship papers before leaving Astoria, and had been a loyal citizen of his adopted country since Civil War days, still he was unable to obtain any of his money from America during his stay in Germany. He did, however, receive his Army pension check. Because of his extended absence from the United States, and one might say because of the war hysteria, he was declared an alien by the United States Government, and his property confiscated. After the war was over he was permitted to return to Astoria, where his citizenship and property rights were restored.

German-born August Scherneckau's name was corrupted by his Indian friends to Shaniko.

Scherneckau built a store, saloon, and a 16-room inn at Cross Hollows.

When he returned to America he was accompanied by his sister. They moved to Santa Monica, California. He died there at the age of 86. His ashes were buried at the Oceanview Cemetery in Astoria in a plot set aside for soldiers of the Grand Army of the Republic. Beneath a canopy of branches can be found the thin, weatherbeaten slab with the fading inscription: A. Scherneckau, Co. H 1 Nebraska Cavalry.

2

ROUND-UP AND BAKEOVEN

Horse Racing at Round-up Time

The canyons beginning at Cross Hollows fed from one into another, finally emptying into the John Day River, then on to the Columbia. These miles of canyons became excellent range land for the ranchers in Greater Wasco County, which at that time stretched east into Idaho and included land that now comprises Sherman County. Will Guyton lived about 17 miles from Cross Hollows. With other boys he got work riding this range for the ranchers on the breaks of the canyons. In 1887, Will made his first ride in the roundup. Later he described his memory of that ride:

"I started working in the round-up before I was sixteen. I worked in it for Muddy Company, Macken, and for Mike and Tom Glavey for the biggest part of two years, rounding up stock. I met the horse roundup in front of what is now Arthur Schmidt's place. We started at Bakeoven and later camped at Henry Rooper's near Antelope. Everyone who had horses helped with the roundup. I wasn't herding, but riding—hunting horses. Everyone joined the roundup when it got in the vicinity of their place and when their stock was all in a corral they took them and went home.

Charley Durbin was a great fellow—prided himself in having the best saddle horses in the country. I was breaking saddle horses for Jimmy Macken. Charley Durbin came and rode one day. He was bragging about his horse.

Ernie Kimsey was there. I was late getting out of Cove (on the Deschutes) and it was hot. Ernie came over to help me in. He said, "Bill can that horse run?" I said, "Macken horses ain't race horses." He was riding one of old Charley's horses. "Let's race them," he said.

We did and later in camp, Ernie sidled over and listened to Charley spout about his horses, then said, "Damned if I think your horse can run so fast. I've $5 that says this horse

Cowboys didn't always wear blue jeans. Claud Guyton dressed up to go to town. A spirited horse and good outfit were the forerunners of the ethos of sports car ownership. When riding the range a good horse was absolutely essential to a cowboy. A well-trained horse knew when to cut an animal out of a group or prevent one from leaving the band of horses or herd of cattle; he made his move even before his rider signaled with knee pressure or change of bridle reins. Man and horse at their best, were as one.

of Macken's can beat him." Charley put up a $5 gold piece. Ernie rode my horse and won. Charley was so mad he about split when Ernie told him he'd already run them.

"I homesteaded between Shaniko and Kent just north of the present Sherman-Wasco County line. My "Dad"— W.F. Guyton—and I bought a lot of horses from Macken for $3,000. Macken had been in the business for 40 years (about 1854 to 1894). Dad and I gathered 320 head of horses the first roundup from John Day River to Deschutes and Antelope to Grass Valley. Macken's brand was "JM." There were so many people that had "JM" horses that I got to using "A/" brand on the hip. You had to keep riding all the time to keep colts branded before someone else slapped a brand on them.

The Homestead Act

In 1862, the Congress of the United States passed the Homestead Act. Under provisions of the act, anyone 21 years old or head of a family could acquire by settlement and improvement, a title to 160 acres of public land. This first Homestead Act encouraged further settlement of public lands, particularly in the West. Even aliens who filed intention of becoming citizens were entitled to take up homesteads. A large number of Germans, Swiss, Irish, Scotch, and English immigrants settled in Central Oregon.

The only payment required was a small administrative fee. The homesteader was required to live on the land five years and to improve it as a residence. The five years could be shortened by paying $1.25 an acre after 14 months, or $2.50 an acre if the land was situated within United States Railroad Grants.

It was not many years until the fertile land in southern Wasco County was under cultivation and good homes were built near the source of water in the canyons. During the early years the ranchers used the unfenced land around them to graze sheep. Each year they increased the number of bands they owned, and when the wool and lambs were sold they bought more land, until a few of the early homesteaders became large land-holders with many bands of sheep.

In 1905, the Homestead Act was enlarged, but since there was no longer land in the public domain that was suitable for farming, the size of free homestead sites was increased to 320 acres. The grazing land that had been available for the early ranchers was being fenced off and they came to depend on the National Forest Land for summer range, which meant trailing the bands of sheep long distances in the spring and fall.

Even 320 acres of bunchgrass on the hills did not produce enough income to support a family, so some of the new homesteaders abandoned their claims and went home. In 1901, a Bakeoven student writing to her teacher said, "The land is all settled up with homesteaders around here now. I don't see what those people live on, there is absolutely nothing to stay there for—there is neither wood nor water."

Some of them left their claims, some lived on their land the required six months of the year, made the minimum required improvements, and sold the land to nearby ranchers once the claim was "proved up on."

But for all the hardships, people came to claim the land. The influx of homesteaders along with the building of the first railroad line into the interior of the State of Oregon, brought about a veritable explosion of people to southern Wasco County.

Bakeoven

At the time when Cross Hollows Station was a successful business enterprise under the management of August Scherneckau, a similar stage station at Bakeoven was providing services for the heavy road traffic. In 1871, Joseph Henry

Even 320 acres of bunchgrass did not provide income to support a family, so some homesteaders abandoned their claims. Not so, Mary Wakerlig, who said, "No one can know how dear a homestead cabin can be until he doesn't have a home."

Sherar homesteaded the land on which Bakeoven stage stop and camping spot were located. In 1872, Andy Swift established the Bakeoven Inn, blacksmith shop, and livery barn, so freighters and travelers would have a place to spend the night, feed their horses and make repairs on their wagons after the rough travel from The Dalles. He operated this important station until 1873 when he sold it to Thomas Burgess.

Tom had followed gold mining from California to Idaho and back to Oregon before he married Ella Smith of The Dalles and settled down to keep the Bakeoven stage-stop. The Burgesses were friendly, generous people who soon became well known in Central Oregon for their hospitality and for the quality of the food they served.

Burgess bought more land and improved the many-roomed ranch house so he could offer comfortable overnight accommodations. The barn was enlarged for the shelter of more horses and the storage of hay and grain to

Burgess improved the many-roomed house and enlarged the barn, before he sold to Henry Wakerlig. Wakerlig family in foreground.

Buildings at Bakeoven. Blacksmith shop at extreme right. "They put benches in a hall over the blacksmith shop for a schoolhouse." It was also a place for social gatherings, dances and church services. See railing leading to hall.

Blacksmith shop on left, and other Bakeoven buildings.

feed them. The blacksmith shop was ready to repair wagons and harness. Because of the hard labor of Tom and Ellen Burgess, the station became fairly self-sufficient. They planted fruit trees, raised a large garden on the fertile sub-irrigated meadow, and worked long hours preparing and cooking the food, in addition to raising and harvesting the feed they provided. They employed young men to do much of the farm work as well as young girls to help in the kitchen.

They built a large hall over the blacksmith shop which became a place for social affairs. On a Saturday night there was often dancing; on a Sunday morning if a preacher were available, there was a church service. People came in their hacks, buggies, or wagons from nearby ranches and homesteads.

In December 1875, the Bakeoven Post Office opened for business with Mrs. Burgess as the first postmaster—adding another chore to her already heavy work load.

It was miles to some of the surrounding ranches and homes, but the services rendered by the Burgesses created a center for the community round about, bringing the neighbors to Bakeoven to buy supplies, have horses shod, receive the mail, and exchange local news. The Burgesses remained at the Bakeoven Station nearly 30 years before retiring to The Dalles in 1902. By that time the community was well established and has continued to be a recognized rural entity.

Solomon Hauser

Solomon Hauser, one of the first sheep kings of the Bakeoven country, was born in Switzerland, but came to Wasco County before he married. He owned a ranch near Bakeoven and several bands of sheep before he sent for Susetta Wakerlig to be his wife. He met her in The Dalles and they were married at the Blaser home. They had two children, Solomon and Rose.

Hauser had a large corral at Tygh Valley as well as the one at Bakeoven. He was in France on business when word reached him that the scab had infected many flocks of sheep in Wasco County. He hurried home to treat his sheep. A dipping vat was built at Bakeoven near the Alden place, and another at Tygh Valley, and he saved his herds.

In November 1895, Hauser went out on the hills to hunt sheep and got caught in a storm. He had so much difficulty finding his way home that he was chilled through and died with pneumonia. He owned six bands of sheep (1,000 to a band) at the time.

When his nephew, K. L. Lohrli, in Switzerland heard of his uncle's death, he came to Oregon to assist Mrs. Hauser with the ranching operations. They were later married and had two children, Clara and Conrad. Mr. Lohrli took the name of Hauser, though those who knew him well spoke of him as "K.L."

Bakeoven School

As time went on, the homesteaders and ranchers around Bakeoven decided their children should have an education, so they took up a subscription to hire a teacher for two three-month terms a year. Then they put benches in a vacant building located above the inn, for a schoolhouse. The Superintendent of Public Instruction at The Dalles provided examinations to certify anyone who applied for a position as teacher in a rural school. The tests were on the following subjects: Orthography, Reading, Writing, Geography, Mental Arithmetic, Written Arithmetic, English Grammar, Modern History, Physiology & Hygiene, Theory of Teaching, Civil Government, and School Law. In March of 1897, Ada Bell, a 16-year-old girl from Boyd, near The Dalles, took the examinations and passed with a general average of 94½, so was certified to teach at Bakeoven.

Since there was no place for the teacher to live, it was necessary for her to live around in the different homes of her pupils during the three-month term. Ada wrote of her teaching experience: "Bakeoven was 40 miles away from home, and it took all day on the stage to get there. I had only $4.00 to buy my ticket. When I got off the stage, there was no one there to meet me, and I was frightened. The driver offered to lend me the money for my night's lodging, but I said I'd ask Mrs. Burgess to trust me, and she did. The next afternoon, Mrs. William Kelsay came for me and I boarded with her. I had, at first, seven pupils, Rosa, Ernest, Julia, and Anna Wakerlig; Leo and Jesse Fleming, and Martha Borstel."

Ada attended high school in The Dalles between terms of teaching at Bakeoven. In a theme written later, on the subject of her first day teaching school, she said, "I had wondered what my first day at school would be like. I'd heard stories in which pupils had formed plans for shutting the teacher out of the school room, or had hidden snakes or lizards in her desk. I was anxious and nervous that first morning. When I

Left: Solomon Hauser was one of the first cattle kings of the Bakeoven area. His children Solomon and Rose, were taught by Ada Bell. *Right:* When K.L. Lohrli heard of his uncle Solomon Hauser's death, he came to the United States to help Mrs. Hauser operate the ranch. Later, he married Mrs. Hauser and took the name of Hauser. Their children, Clara and Conrad, with their parents.

Left: In 1901 Ada Bell graduated from The Dalles High School.
Right: Ada Bell, a 16-year-old girl from Boyd, near The Dalles, took the teacher's examination and passed with a general average of over 94, so was hired to teach at Bakeoven.

Henry Wakerlig, homesteader sheepman.

reached the school house I found the door wired shut. I was
puzzled, but soon unfastened it, and the door swung open.

"I had attended a country school, but nothing like this! I
remembered the delightful school room which fancy had
portrayed, but never once had I imagined myself teaching in
a room like this one: large rude desks, the floor and walls
were of rough wood—no ceiling, and only three half-win-
dows. Bits of paper and chalk were scattered about while
dust reigned supremely over all. I hastily swept the floor and
tried to put on the expression of a teacher with years of experience, when I saw the children coming up the walk. I managed to articulate a faint "Good Morning" as each child
entered the room. By the time it was nine o'clock I felt better. These pupils were not the ones of whom I had fondly
dreamed, but they had intelligent minds, and I'd help them
to learn and be happy."

Ada Bell taught five different three-month terms at Bakeoven.

Henry Wakerlig

In 1898, Burgess sold the Bakeoven holdings to Henry
Wakerlig, who with his large family contributed much to the
life and interest of both Bakeoven and Shaniko. Henry Wakerlig and Maria Witweiler, his wife, left Switzerland for
Canada in November of 1882. In October of the following

year, they arrived in The Dalles, according to Wakerlig, with five children and $3, not enough to pay freight on their baggage. He was a man who could be trusted, and on promise to pay later, he took his baggage and went to his wife's relative, Solomon Hauser, in the Bakeoven area.

Hauser had several bands of sheep, so Henry herded until the spring of 1884, when he moved to Cross Hollows, rented a house from Mr. Scherneckau for his family, then went to Antelope to herd sheep for Al Porter. After two years, Wakerlig bought 400 head of sheep from Scherneckau. Here is his account of the following years: "Moved to Paulina Valley with my family, lost half of my sheep. In the fall of 1887 went back to Cross Hollows. In the spring of 1888 went to Ochoco Gulch (Bakeoven vicinity) to take a homestead. In the fall of 1889 had 2800 head of sheep, but lost 2400 that bad winter. Four thousand dollars in debt, started again with remainder of sheep, had all my debts paid in 1898.

"In 1902, I bought Bakeoven Ranch. In 1906, had 10,000 head of sheep. Also in 1906, seven members of the family had typhoid fever. Mother and Rosa died. Sold out to William Moody, May 13, 1912."

This terse account of Wakerlig's struggle in the sheep business is fairly typical. He stayed with it long enough to make considerable money, perhaps somewhat at the expense of his large family, for there were 11 children born to Henry and Mary Wakerlig. The older ones had little education, but the younger ones did attend grade school at Bakeoven.

Was an Oven Really Built at Bakeoven?

There is some difference of opinion concerning the origin of the name Bakeoven, first spelled Bake Oven, as two words. Most historians tell a story which runs something like this: "Henry Sherar, on his way to Canyon City, camped overnight in the canyon where there was water for the horses. He was accompanied by a Frenchman hauling a load of flour to sell in Canyon City, who may have expected to bake bread and sell there. That night some Indians drove off his horses and left him stranded without transportaion. He constructed a rough clay and stone bake oven. He was there several weeks, salvaging his flour and his investment by baking bread for other travelers who came by, before he could get horses to continue his journey. The oven was often used by later parties, so the place became known as Bake Oven."

Julia Wakerlig was a little girl when her father bought Bakeoven Ranch and she well remembered hearing Tom Burgess "tell it like it was," in her words. She recalls going down the canyon "a ways" to a place scooped out of the rock bank, where branches were burned to heat a crude oven. Julia said, "There never was any oven at the ranch. A man had homesteaded where the buildings are now and nothing else. Looking straight down from the schoolhouse, you could still see the wagon tracks when we moved there, and the dugout in the hill. That Frenchman built a front on it like those old-time cellars. Every night he made this dough and put it in seven iron Dutch ovens. Every morning he put it in to bake."

At any rate, Bake Oven it became, and while the early buildings have all disappeared, there is now a ranch house, with a barn and other small farm buildings in the canyon of the community which continues to be known as Bakeoven.

Richard Roland Hinton

Richard R. Hinton, a man who drastically altered the homesteading scene in southern Wasco County arrived with a pack horse, a saddle horse, and a six-shooter—according to his grandson, Bob Hinton. He did ranch work for the early settlers before he took up a homestead adjoining Bakeoven Ranch.

R.R. Hinton was born in Missouri in 1852 of English and Irish parents who had moved to Missouri from Alabama.

When he was a boy, they moved again to Lane County, Oregon. Some time after he took his Bakeoven homestead, he married Mary Emma "Maria" Fitzpatrick (1873.) During the first year of their marriage, money was scarce and they lived in a cave dug out of the bank about two miles down-canyon from the place where the present Hinton ranch house stands. Maria stitched deerskin gloves and sold them whenever anyone was found with money to buy them. This helped provide such staples as salt, sugar and flour.

On January 6, 1874, James E. Hinton, their son, was born in that dugout room.

Before many years Hinton had accumulated several bands of sheep. He built a home and moved his family to the present ranch site; and he bought out many homesteads until, eventually, he owned 15,000 acres of wheat and pasture land that became known as the Imperial Stock Ranch. He ordered breeding stock of cattle and horses from England.

Besides James E., the Hintons had a daughter, Lillian (Hollingshead). While the children were fairly young, the Burgesses and Hintons neighbored back and forth. One time, when Mrs. Hinton was sick, Mrs. Burgess came to see what she could do for her. She found her very ill. Mrs. Hinton kept trying to tell Mrs. Burgess something, perhaps about the children, but was never able to say what she wished to. Mrs. Hinton died that night, and was buried not far from the house on the home ranch, in a place that has since come to be known as the Hinton Cemetery. It holds the graves of numerous relatives, friends and others.

German Families

A number of German families immigrated to the Bakeoven area in the 1890's. Among them were the von Borstels, Reckmans, Detjens, and Patjens. One of the Patjens boys, Andy, was to vie with Hinton and Wakerlig in buying up homestead land around Bakeoven. Patjens' main wheat ranch

R.R. Hinton and his second wife, Mary Ann Bird. Mrs. Hinton became worried and distraught about her daughter's untimely death, and finally committed suicide.

Home of R.R. Hinton, owner of Imperial Stock Ranch near Bakeoven.

A number of German families immigrated to Bakeoven area. Among them was the Patjens family. One of the Patjens boys, Andy, was to vie with Hinton and Wakerlig in buying up homesteads in the vicinity. *Left to right back row:* Andy, Adele Meyer Patjens, Otto Dethlefs. *Front row:* Ernest and Andy Patjens.

Trailing sheep to the mountains near upper Deschutes River (Oregon Historical Society picture). One year Jim Hinton trailed 2,000 head of sheep all the way to Wyoming, fording rivers. The sheep could swim, buoyed up by their fluffy wool.

was made up of homesteads bought from Bauman, Boatman, Burke, Dairs, Kirkpatrick, Pratt, Rogers, Sayers, Theis Weidewitz, Wilson, and Yeakey. He bought considerably more land as well as other homesteads, which made up the central eastern part of his ranch holdings. One of his sons, Ernest, now raises beef cattle on the land accumulated by his father. The other, Andy H., lives with his wife in Bella Vista, Arkansas.

James E. Hinton—Rancher and Sheepman

James E. Hinton, born in that dugout cave in a hillside at Bakeoven, grew up on the Imperial Stock Ranch. He attended Hill Military Academy in Portland, then returned to Bakeoven to "pack" for his father in the summers. He was considered one of the best and most efficient packers in Central Oregon. He knew how to load pack horses and to tie large loads securely on their backs. He had the reputation of keeping the herders well supplied with necessities before it was possible to haul supplies by truck. He also herded sheep to the mountains on occasion.

One year Jim trailed 2,000 head of sheep all the way to Wyoming. The sheep forded the rivers, buoyed up by their fluffy wool. He had expected to settle there, but it was the time of the sheep and cattlemen's war, so he shipped the sheep on to Chicago to market by train. He came back to the Bakeoven area and bought the Maxwell place, then the Newcomb place, and finally, one at Dead Dog near Maupin.

In 1913, Jim Hinton bought out his father, R.R. Hinton, who owned about 15,000 acres at that time. R.R. moved to La Jolla, California. In the winter of 1930 he returned to Portland. He died there a few years later.

Jim Hinton himself became a large land owner, adding thousands of acres to the ranch of his father. According to the 1945 Oregon Census, he owned the largest unincorporated sheep and cattle ranch in Oregon. He was the sole

Haystack on the J.E. Hinton ranch. Nothing was done in a small way, even the haystacks were gigantic.

owner of 200,000 acres of land. He was then paying the single highest farm property tax in Oregon. Among the homesteads he bought in the Bakeoven vicinity were the Higgins, Harris, Maxwell Canyon Ranch, Ewen McLennan and Chandler land, as well as Bakeoven Ranch which he bought from Clara Moody. He traded, and received mail in Shaniko. The first year the Forest Service issued permits for grazing on National Forest lands, 1905, J.E. Hinton received a permit for the pasture of 9,600 head of grown sheep and lambs.

In about 1940, J.E. Hinton sold a partnership interest in his holdings to George Ward, and the Imperial Stock Ranch built up by R.R. Hinton became known as the Hinton-Ward Ranch. J.E. Hinton retired and he and his wife moved to Salem to live; after her death he moved to California. His mind remained clear as long as he lived. He was 98 when he died. (Born Jan. 6, 1873; died 1971)

Wool

At a time when wool represented universal protection from cold, the thousands of square miles of range lands of Eastern Oregon were ideally suited to produce wool. Sheep are practical animals, able to traverse uneven and rocky terrain without fatigue or mishap. One difficulty for sheepmen was getting feed to their flocks when snow covered the ground, so as Henry Wakerlig related, many sheep were lost before ranchers were able to build shelters for the severe winters, or store hay for feed. Freighters hauled out pelts in the spring after the severe winters took their toll. Even in the summer there were hazards to be encountered. In 1902, a forest fire swept over the range in the mountains and two thousand sheep were lost in one band, and the lives of the herders were endangered.

Sheepherders lived a lonely life. For months sometimes, they saw only the driver of the supply wagon. Camp gear provided the only shelter, and companionship was furnished by a faithful sheep dog. Of the German, Swiss, and Irish sheepmen who eventually owned large bands, some like Wakerlig, began with very little credit, no money, and much determination. Some herders, liking the quiet life and simple mode of living, spent their lives herding sheep.

3

COMING OF THE RAILROAD

In March of 1897, the same year that Ada Bell first taught at Bakeoven, the Columbia Southern Railway Company filed incorporation papers stating their intent to build a railroad from the Columbia River south into Central Oregon. The first stirrings came from local businessmen of The Dalles and northern Sherman County. Later the company received some financial backing from Oregon Railway and Navigation Company.

Farmers of Sherman County were so eager for the coming of good rail transportation that they worked their own teams and fresnos (large scoops) in the construction of the first miles of line as far as Moro.

When the decision was made to extend the line from Moro south, there was again cooperation and excitement among ranchers and stockmen along the proposed route. Small towns prepared for the growth they felt sure would follow the railroad to their community. Suddenly the place where the railroad was to terminate was under scrutiny. There was little there except the memory of the importance of Cross Hollows as a freight and passenger stop during the gold rush to Canyon City. That memory took on significance when some of the same men from The Dalles and Moro, who incorporated to build the railroad, formed what was to be known as "The Townsite Company." They were reported to have had capital of $48,000 to acquire land at the rail terminal and prepare a town for the coming of the railroad. This company was made up of B.F. Laughlin, E.C. Pease, D.M. French,

J.W. French, W. Lord—all of The Dalles and W.H. and H.A. Moore of Moro.

In October 1899, Townsite Company bought ground on the hill above Cross Hollows, from W.H. Moore and his wife for $3,500, the NE Quarter ¼ Section Number One, Township 7 South. They laid out streets for a town, then arranged for the installation of a water system, utilizing the fresh, cool water which was abundant at Cross Hollows. So confident were they that in January 1900, they advertised in the *Morning Oregonian* that the Columbia Southern Railway would be completed to Shaniko by April 1, 1900. In this advertisement, the company stated that Shaniko was destined to become the largest wool market in the world. They determined that the name of the new city would be "Shaniko," the old Indian pronunciation of the name Scherneckau, in honor of the prosperous German, the former stage-stop keeper at Cross Hollows, just over the brow of the hill from the end of the rail line.

When the first passenger train arrived in Shaniko in May, of 1900, there was a city to greet the waving train crew—a tent city, which was housing the many men employed in construction work. The new metropolis-in-the-making had incorporated in February 1900. The Federal Census of June 1, 1900, gave the population of Shaniko as 172, mostly construction workers.

Two of the early Columbia Southern backers from The Dalles, B.F. Laughlin and W. Lord, filed incorporation papers in late September 1899, with a capital of $42,000 to build a warehouse at Shaniko. It was completed in 1901. Other storage buildings followed. Shaniko Warehouse could store 4,000,000 pounds of wool, and all the wheat arriving. The company also handled building materials, fence posts, and fuel (coal and wood).

Almost before the buildings were completed, freight wagons began coming in to unload wool and wheat on the long loading dock. As the train brought in freight, this was un-

Shaniko in 1901 - The tent city begins to give way to more permanent structures. Wiley's saloon in center, Pease & Mays store in left center back, water tower to right. The second building from the left is Townsite Building.

Building the Shaniko Warehouse in about 1901. Considered the most extensive wool warehouse in the State, it contained room to store four million pounds of wool and all the wheat that came in at that time.

loaded on the opposite side of the building and picked up by wagons and drays ready to make the long trip out to the interior of the state.

People were arriving on the train daily to seek work, to buy, or to sell. Many of them hired rigs or saddle horses to continue their travel to other communities. All of this required the building of livery stables and feed lots. Eventually, there were four large stables and several feed lots in scattered locations around town, which held the incoming sheep and carloads of cattle waiting for shipment to market or summer range. Special trains of 50 cars or more moved the sheep to their destination.

The Columbia Southern Railroad Company itself was expanding. In 1902, railroad shops were completed, ready to repair equipment and keep engines running efficiently. In 1903, there were offices representing the company in Moro and Portland, besides the main office in Shaniko, which had six officers in addition to fifteen other persons working for the company. It is estimated that railroad business alone added 80 people to the town's population of 300.

In 1902, there were 400 cars of cattle shipped out to market. The Shaniko Warehouse was considered the most extensive wool warehouse in the state, and there were other business people ready to establish connections in the new city. In 1900 the Moody Warehouse Company in The Dalles had sent William A. Rees to Shaniko to attend the wool sale and to bid on some of the clips (fleeces). The following year this company also built a warehouse (covering 75,000 square feet) in Shaniko. Former Governor Zenas Moody—who owned the company of that name in The Dalles—sent his son William H. to manage the new warehouse. Up until that time, Moody Warehouse Company in The Dalles had been conducting a commission business in Shaniko.

As time went on, separate buildings were made ready to store hay, coal, and kerosene, in addition to the barley warehouse with its steam-rolling plant where wheat, barley

Almost before the warehouse buildings were completed, wagons lined up at the long loading dock. For wool hauling, typically, three wagons pulled by six or eight horses were used. Wool was 20c per pound. Sometimes the producers hired commercial haulers, sometimes they hauled their own wool. Occasionally homesteaders picked up a little bit of cash by doing outside hauling.

Local farmers hauled their smaller yield of wool to the warehouse, or hauled for other people, just as Dave Wilson did in 1914.

SHANIKO DEPOT IN 1910

The Columbia Southern Line was expanding. A substantial Depot was built.

and oats were processed for feed. Slabwood was piled outside after being sawed up to appropriate lengths. A lumber yard was located beneath the southern end of the large wool warehouse.

From the day in 1901 when the first train reached Shaniko, the future of the city appeared assured. For the first time in history, rail transportation was within reach of isolated stock and wheat producers in the inland reaches of Oregon. Ranchers and farmers had long needed a way out to market. When the rails finally reached the terminal at Shaniko, it was agreed that shipping by train surely beat trailing stock all the way out on foot.

The trains carried more than stock and produce. The hotels, streets, and saloons in Shaniko were often crowded with the drummers who came to sell their wares, the visitors, the travelers to Oregon's outback, and the buyers of cattle, sheep, wool, and wheat. There was money to be made by almost everyone.

But for the trains it wasn't easy. The rails climbed a grade total of over 3,000 feet from Biggs to Shaniko. At times it was necessary for the engine to "double-back," hauling half

Columbia Southern Schedule
Biggs to Shaniko
Time Table No. 8
Effective 12:01 a.m. Sept 9, 1900

1st Class Southbound	STATIONS Daily Pass'r	1st Class Northbound
No. 2 Leave P.M.		No. 1 Arrive A.M.
1:34	Biggs	11:25
1:59	Gibsons	11:00
2:14	Wasco	10:45
2:27	Klondyke	10:30
2:33	Summit	10:25
2:45	Hay Can. Jct.	10:15
2:48	McDonalds	10:12
3:00	DeMoss	10:00
3:09	Moro	9:50
3:19	Erskinville	9:39
3:44	Grass Valley	9:15
4:06	Bourbon	8:55
4:26	Kent	8:40
4:40	Wilcox	8:30
5:20	SHANIKO	8:00

P.M.	A.M.
Arrive	Leave
D.J. Harris	C.E. Lytle
Superintendent	G.P. Agent

the cars to Moro, then returning to Biggs for the rest. Sometimes floods caused delays. In March of 1910, there were severe wash-outs between Biggs and Wasco. One winter the snow delayed the train so long that 30 issues of the daily newspapers and back-logged mail were delivered in Shaniko at one time, probably January of 1916.

At that time, the passenger train was caught between Wilcox and Shaniko, then rescued by a work train. In the second week of December 1919, the train could not get above Grass Valley. Snowplows were often brought up to clear the tracks. For three days after the great snow of November 1921, which produced huge drifts near Thornberry, the line was blocked. In February 1923, the engine plowed with difficulty through eight-foot drifts in the cuts south of Moro.

But for all the difficulties encountered in maintianing rail service, it is said the Biggs-Shaniko line was one of the most productive branch lines in the United States.

J.J. Wiley, Saloon-keeper

J.J. Wiley was managing the saloon at the City Hotel Inn in Moro when the Columbia Southern train made its maiden entrance into that town, December 14, 1898, amid the ringing of bells, the whistle of the locomotive, the firing of anvils, and the cheering of excited citizens. Wiley was not one to miss a golden opportunity, so when word was out that the train line would terminate at Cross Hollows 39 miles south of Moro, he was there ahead of time with his tent set up and plenty of whiskey on hand as the workers arrived. The first wooden structure in the new town of Shaniko was the small saloon built by J.J. Wiley. No doubt he officiated at the bar in that saloon when the first work train puffed into Shaniko on an April day in 1900. No record has been found of the celebration planned or the welcome given the train crew, but it is a guess that it was loud and enthusiastic—and alcoholic.

The first wooden structure in the new town of Shaniko was a small saloon built by Julius J. Wiley. When the first work train puffed into Shaniko that April Day in 1900, he was likely officiating at the bar "setting them up."

Weather finally settled the fate of the Columbia Southern Line - now owned by the Union Pacific Railroad Company - in December 1964 when an unusually heavy snow fell, followed by chinook winds, then rain. The streams overflowed their banks, and when the flood waters reached northern Sherman County, the creek had become a raging river, washing out the railroad tracks and roadbed. In Biggs Canyon the rails lay twisted and scattered. The Union Pacific Railroad branch line through Sherman County was no more.

Wiley petitioned for a saloon license, Sept. 10, 1901, one of the earliest licenses granted for the sale of liquor in less than quart amounts. The last renewal of his license was in April, 1903.

Wiley was active on the council of the City of Shaniko from December 30, 1901, until Feburary 1, 1904, when he asked that the Council accept his resignation. The resignation was accepted and his name does not appear on the books again.

4

TOWN OF HIGH HOPES

Homes

The Townsite Company built the first houses in Shaniko; none of them were large or fine homes. The first house was a rectangular two-story structure of 20' x 80'; it served as living quarters for the officials of the company. Office space was on the ground floor. After that building was finished, workmen hastily constructed the first of the family residences. These houses were occupied as soon as ready by the business and professional people, whose families were often waiting in The Dalles or some other place with relatives until housing was available. Often, two families occupied one house.

The business people who arrived in Shaniko had come from established communities. Their lives were quite different from those of the homesteaders and immigrants. Though their homes were not elegant, they made them as comfortable and attractive as possible. For instance, the house the Moodys lived in was furnished with books, art objects and substantial furnishings.

The Water Tower and Water Works

The townspeople called the huge water-storage structure built west of town the "water tower." There were two 10,000 gallon tanks suspended 70 feet above the ground high enough for gravity flow to reach all the buildings in town. Townsite Company boxed up the larger springs at Cross Hollows with cement and piped the water down the canyon to a huge storage reservoir. From the reservoir in the canyon a steam engine pumped the water to the tower on the hill. A wood fire heated the boiler to power the steam engine. There was a bounteous supply of fresh, clear water to keep the tanks filled.

The whole system was completed, the mains laid, and connections at the building sites were ready for the new city by July 1900, at a cost of $20,000.

History of the Water Works

In 1913, a special session of the City Council was called to discuss the purchase of the City Water Works, "Watco." Townsite Company agreed to the $3,000 offered for the plant, the acreage containing the springs, and the engineer's residence. (The pump man was to be paid $60 a month.) The deal was finalized a few days later.

The rate schedule for the Railroad Company was 40c per 1,000 gallons on metered pipes and $5 a month for water delivered to the depot. For townspeople the rate was $5 for each hydrant in use during the three summer months and a monthly house fee of $2.50.

In 1920, the old steam pumping system was considered inadequate, so in April of that year the council voted to purchase a diesel engine from Fairbanks Morse Company of Portland; $500 was paid on the contract price of $2,280. This contract was retired in 1927. The new diesel motor was started by heating the cylinder with a blow-torch. When the cylinder was hot it was necessary to step on the spoke of a huge flywheel to start it in action.

In late 1943, when the Rural Electrification lines reached Shaniko, an electric motor pump was ordered to replace the huge diesel motor and flywheel that were still in use. When the new motor, not quite four feet long, arrived, it looked so small in contrast that the pump man Gus Reeder was taken aback, "It'll never do it!" he exclaimed. "It will never pump the water up there!"—and he threw his hat on the ground in frustration; but when the connections were completed the new small motor pump easily raised the water up to the storage tower on the hill.

The Columbia Southern Hotel

The Townsite Company planned to build a fine hotel in Shaniko that would equal if not exceed the comforts offered by the Umatilla House in The Dalles, one of the finest inns in Central Oregon. The contractor hired for the work was Fredrick Schilling, who set up a kiln and made the bricks in the canyon below Kelsey Springs, several miles north of Shaniko. The first train to reach town carried these bricks and the lumber for the construction of the building.

The owner, Mr. Fen Batty, who had managed the Umatilla House in The Dalles, opened the establishment for service in December of 1901. J.M. Keeney was the first manager.

In 1904, Joseph Batty purchased the Columbia Southern Hotel from his brother, Fen, but the following year, 1905, he sold it to J.M. Keeney for $8,000. Keeney continued to operate it from 1905 until May 29, 1911, when he sold out to Archie Mason and left Shaniko. Thereafter, the property changed hands frequently. From Mason, it went to C.R. Creamer, to W.T. Krebs, then to J.O. Elrod, and after that to Mabel Hinkson. In 1920, E.H. and V.H. French took it over, then sold to Marco Investment Company, who in 1921 sold to W. Dorres.

Townsite Company built a fine hotel that would equal or exceed the comforts offered by the Umatilla House in The Dalles, one of the finest inns in Central Oregon. (Oregon Historical Society Picture)

In May of 1921, Dorres sold the (by then) Shaniko Hotel to John McLennan. During all this time there had been a succession of administrators. Several years after he bought the hotel, John McLennan retired to live there.

Joe and Sue Morelli become managers of the hotel for McLennan in 1954, and in 1955 bought the property.

Literally in the center of town, and certainly because of its early acceptance as The Finest Hotel in Central Oregon, the Columbia Southern Hotel became the scene of many and varied activities for nearly 80 years. Almost before the structure was complete, some space was used by the Pease & Mays department store. An old photo shows a Pease & Mays sign over a door on the east face. Those same rooms once housed the bank, then eventually, a lunch counter. The barroom became a dining room at the time of prohibition. The spacious dining room was often cleared for ballroom dancing, and the lobby became a meeting place for friends, guests, and newcomers.

On the south side of the building, an area that was originally the dining room became the permanent home of Eastern Oregon Banking Company, until the Great Depression closed the bank.

Workers and building materials were sent to Shaniko by train in 1910 and 1911, to be transported to the work sites in the vicinity of Maupin where the Oregon Trunk Railroad Line was being built up the Deschutes River. Some of these people were quartered and spent week-ends in town. There was then not enough hotel space to accommodate the many men coming into town, so the old Townsite Building which had stood near the Shaniko Warehouse, was moved adjacent to the Columbia Southern Hotel's north end, and an opening was cut in the upper hotel wall to open a hallway connecting the two buildings. Room charge for the annex was 25c a night. It was torn down in the 1920's.

The niece of Fen Batty, Alice Sanford (Mrs. Roy McCallister) related her memories of the early days of 1901 when she lived in Shaniko:

Uncle Fen's Hotel
by
Mrs. Roy McAllister

"What exciting times there were for a small girl at the hotel, with prominent personages often stopping. I was there when the Chinese princess in her beautiful bejeweled chair was carried into the lobby. To me, her clothes appeared exotic and like a fairy tale. Her oddly shaped shoes, all gold and jeweled, were never made for walking.

"Uncle Fen must have loved the Chinese people, for two always worked for him in the kitchen and he installed a laundry in Shaniko, run by Chinese. They always made the Chinese New Year seem like another Christmas for us children, when the camphor-wood chest arrived, filled to the brim with foreign silks, foods and dishes.

"I was there when Homer Davenport drew pictures for the "drummers and salesmen" and also when a drummer named Kenersley cut out watchface-sized pictures for everyone.

"The men who filled the lobby in years gone by were affluent businessmen, locators of timber claims, homesteads and the like. There was a barroom, but it was "off limits" to a young girl. I know Frenchy Estebennet came from The Dalles to run it. His small son fell out of an upstairs window onto the boardwalk. The boy suffered a fractured arm but didn't miss a day of school.

"We were living in Moro when "Shaniko" seemed to be the byword in all street conversations. Papa (Alfred Sanford) went to the prairie land which surveyors were platting into lots, set up a store in a tent and was in business in Shaniko for several years. His store grew with the town. One of his store buildings is the present museum, across from Uncle Fen's Hotel (the Pastime).

Newspapers

In April of 1900, William Holder purchased *The Leader*, a weekly newspaper which had been published in Moro. He moved the presses to Shaniko and was editor of the paper he called *Shaniko Leader*. A few copies of this paper furnish interesting data concerning business houses in the infant town. Hopes were high and advertisements enthusiastically described services and merchandise available as being "of the very best," which they may have been for those pioneering days in Central Oregon.

Rates for the *Shaniko Leader* were $1.00 a year by subscription or $1.75 with a weekly *Oregonian*. Later, about 1902, Mr. Holder moved the paper back to Moro.

Two other newspapers were printed for short periods, the *Shaniko Republican* in 1906 and *Shaniko Star* in 1911. Little is known about the *Republican* but *Shaniko Star* was printed by E.H. Overman, who was in business at least three years.

Hotel Shaniko

Hotel Shaniko (not to be confused with the Brick structure later called Shaniko Hotel) was first operated by James McHargue. It was a large, wood-frame structure located on the northwest corner of 3d and E streets. In 1903, the building was damaged by a fire which burned a whole block of business houses including a Chinese rooming house called

Eagle Hotel. When the fire was finally extinguished, only smoking rubble was left where many commercial establishments had been built. The workmen who had begun to build houses immediately started clearing the area and rebuilding shops, saloons, and rooming houses.

Business was brisk the following eight years, until the great fire in 1911 burned the wooden Hotel Shaniko, along with most of the rebuilt business district. It was never restored.

Intermittenly through the years, other establishments and residential structures were destroyed by fire. As Julia Wakerlig put it, "When Shaniko died after the rail line went up the Deschutes River, a lot of places sold out to the insurance companies. They closed up shop, moved out, and the place burned down."

Smallpox Epidemic

That same winter of 1903, a smallpox epidemic broke out, causing the death of 25 to 50 people. The exact number was not recorded, possibly because, in the strain on the authorities just to bury the dead and prevent a spread of the disease, no one kept a record. Many of the victims were temporary residents living in hotels and rooming houses. If their names were known, that knowledge has fallen into oblivion. Mr. Gavin is one of the townspeople who helped dig the graves and bury the dead east of town. There was no cemetery then—or later.

Hotel Shaniko - not to be confused with Shaniko Hotel of a later date - was first operated by James McHargue, whose father, James K. McHargue crossed the plains to settle in Brownsville, with the Brown Party. The building was damaged in 1903 by the fire that destroyed most of a block of busines houses.

Hotel Shaniko was repaired and enlarged after the fire.

James McHargue was the first operator of Hotel Shaniko. His wife, Emma, *extreme left*, cooked during the early years. Their children, shown here, *front left*, Margaret Jane, John, Lillie, Claud, Flora "Flo," on her father's lap, James McHargue.

Central Oregon Stages made a regular stop at Hotel Shaniko to pick up passengers.

The first store built by Pease & Mays Company. It had not been long in use until, on Oct. 2, 1902, this 100-square-foot building was destroyed by fire. The stock, and drug store occupying the building, were a total loss.

Wool Capital of the World

In spite of fire and plague, 1903 was the year Shaniko first earned the title "Wool Capital of the World." That was the year that the three wool sales brought in the largest total sale of wool anywhere on record. During the second sale, W.A. Rees banked over a million dollars for Moody Warehouse Company for one day's transactions. That year the wool sales totaled over three million dollars. In addition to that, 2,229 tons of wool, 1,168,866 bushels of wheat, and numerous carloads of stock were shipped out of Shaniko on the Columbia Southern Railroad, making it one of the most financially productive short lines in the United States.

The following year, 1904, it was estimated that over five million dollars worth of wool changed hands, and again the previously earned title was applicable to Shaniko. Figures for the following six years are not available, but it may be assumed that they were equal, if not greater then those recorded.

Wool Sales

In the early days there were as many as three wool sales a year, depending on the arrival in the spring of freight wagon trains from Burns, Silver Lake, Bend, Condon, or from Bridge Creek, Fossil, John Day Valley, and Maupin.

Wool buyers would fix a date to be in Shaniko. A private railroad pullman car brought them to spend a night in town so they would have a full day for examining and bidding on the wool they would buy.

The owners were present (by pre-arrangement) at the warehouse to show their clips. A warehouseman would pull down a sack from the top of the pile and slit it open. Buyers took out a fleece, separated a handful of wool and examined it for texture, staple and shrinkage. If it was very greasy, it would shrink a lot; grease gathers dirt.

Buyers bid on the wool that best suited their purpose, according to the use planned for it. The bidding was done by sealed bids handed to the warehouse foreman, who talked it over with the owner to see if the offer was acceptable. If agreeable, the owner received a check, his transaction was concluded, and he went to settle up his accounts in town, he then either stopped for refreshments—or left immediately for the long drive to his ranch.

After the wool sale was over, the buyers boarded the pullman and departed on the morning train, leaving the wool in the warehouse to be baled, marked, and loaded in boxcars for shipment to its destination.

A story has been told concerning a very confident wool buyer who appeared at one of the big wool sales in Shaniko. He bragged that he would get just the clip—one man's yearly yield—he chose, and at his own price. When pressed for an explanation he revealed that he carried a million dollars cash in his pocket, "And that is better than any check," he said. According to the story, he got the clips he chose.

Freighters on the way to Silver Lake. These large wagons when loaded, were drawn by six, eight, or even ten horses.

There were often three wool sales a year in the spring, depending on the time freight wagon-trains could reach Shaniko from Burns, Silver Lake, Bend, Condon, or from Bridge Creek, Fossil, John Day Valley and Maupin. (Oregon Historical Society Photo)

Wool buyers arrived by pullman car from as far away as Boston and San Francisco. When they went to the warehouse to see the wool, the crew pulled down a sack and slit it open for examination as to texture, staple, and shrinkage. The buyer left a sealed bid with the warehouseman who delivered it to the owner. This picture was taken during a wool sale about 1904. The men with initials are the only ones identified; WAR, Bill Rees - AM, Adelbert Moody - WHM, William Moody.

Some wool from John Day country had considerable sand in it. There was a scouring mill at The Dalles which removed the dirt and grease from the wool before it was shipped. From The Dalles the wool went East by train or west to Portland to be loaded on ships that passed through the Panama Canal or around the Horn to the East Coast. Wool would gain enough weight from moisture en route by boat to pay the freight cost.

Pease & Mays General Merchandise

Early in 1900, Pease & Mays Company of The Dalles began building their fine large store in Shaniko. Edward C. Pease, one of the original members of the Townsite Company was a partner in the pioneer store bearing his name in The Dalles. For special protection from grass fires, county and city building codes required that brick, stone, or concrete be used for construction of the large store building— except that a wooden structure would be permitted if covered with corrugated iron. The latter option was taken. On the outside, the building was finished with ornamental iron facing.

A drugstore was housed in one part of the first floor. The store was stocked with supplies ranging from hardware, clothing and groceries to fine china and French laces. The whole inland area of Central Oregon suddenly had access to a wide range of merchandise.

In October, not long after the stock was all in and business was thriving, a fire broke out at 8 a.m. in the drugstore. The structure and contents were destroyed completely. The carefully worded fire code did not prevent human carelessness.

Before the Pease & Mays store was completed, Bolton Mercantile Company of Antelope had built a large store less than a block away. After the fire, Pease & Mays bought the Mercantile Company store and stock and moved the building across the street facing east. Bolton returned to Antelope.

Pease & Mays re-stocked until their Shaniko merchandise was said to be of a quantity and quality equal to that of their store in The Dalles. Sometimes a patron brought in an order for sufficient supplies to last a year.

Silvertooth Saloon

Felix Silvertooth moved to Antelope in 1880, where he operated the Idle Hour Saloon. By 1901, he and Sim Browder were in partnership, building the Silvertooth Saloon in the new City of Shaniko. They operated saloons in both towns until Felix decided to move to Silver Lake, leaving management of the Silvertooth Saloon to his son John. In 1911, the big fire destroyed their building in Shaniko. There was a fine, old grandfather's clock with mercury weights in the bar. When the fire broke out, the volunteer firemen carried the clock to safety behind the Rees barn nearby and laid it down, causing the large weights by which the clock was wound to lose their quicksilver. There is no way to gather up mercury. It falls into very small beads and disperses; so the clock was ruined.

John Silvertooth continued to manage the Idle Hour Saloon in Antelope until fire destroyed both it and his large collection of rocks, early in the 1960's. John had accumulated antiques and western artifacts as well as his famous rock collection until the space inside and outside the building was filled with his display. The Antelope hills have given up a large variety of agates, thunder eggs, and other collectable rocks.

John was a great story teller. One of his favorite stories concerned the origin of his grandmother, Ella Caleb, mother of Felix Silvertooth and the daughter of an army officer sent west to quiet the Indians in the Oregon Territory. Ella was the first white girl born in Wasco County. John Silvertooth is deceased but his sister, Chattie Silvertooth, lives in Portland.

Livery Stables and Stages

Livery stables and stage lines provided a vital link between
the isolated communities of Central Oregon and the railroad
terminal at Shaniko. Roads were still little more than parallel
tracks in the dirt and clay hillsides in 1901. Drivers, passengers, horses, and harness all suffered from the strain of
jolts and bumps caused by ruts and rocks along the way.
Fatigue lined the faces of guests registering at local hotels
and rooming houses. The horses were fed and cared for in
the livery stables. Harness makers did a thriving business.

Shaniko Stage unloads at Madras.

Four large livery stables were kept busy caring for the teams and saddle horses, as well as renting equipment to newcomers bound for the outlying communities. Early operators of such stables were Randall & Baker, Delmar Howell, John Flanagan, and Chester Ward.

G.M. Cornet operated a line of horse-drawn stages in all directions from Shaniko.

Time Schedule of Cornett Stages

Leaves Shaniko 6 p.m. every day, including Sundays, for Antelope, Cross Keys, Hay Creek, Prineville, and on through via Silver Lake to Klamath Falls.

Leaves Shaniko 6 p.m. for Fossil via Antelope, Tuesdays, Thursdays and Saturdays.

Leaves Shaniko 6 p.m daily except Sunday for Antelope, Mitchell, Dayville and Canyon City.

Leaves Shaniko 6 p.m. for Ashwood, via Antelope on Mondays, Wednesdays and Fridays.

Leaves Shaniko 6 p.m. daily except Sunday for Bakeoven, Sherar's Bridge, Nansene, Boyd and The Dalles.

J.M. KEENEY, Agent, Shaniko

First Inter-city Bus

The first inter-city bus in the United States made it's initial run between Shaniko and Bend. Two dates have been put forth, one in 1905, the other in 1910. It did not become an established run for reasons described by Harry Hill, who witnessed the departure of this early motor-drawn stagecoach:

"The bus started about 9 o'clock in the morning. It consisted of a vehicle with bench seats open at both ends for riders to board from either side. A good portion of the townspeople were present to see this epochal event, and after the word was given and the start made, most of us children ran alongside the bus for some distance. But not for long, as just outside the town the first breakdown occurred. The nature of the failure I don't know, but there was much conversation between the driver and officials accompanying the vehicle. After an hour or so, repairs had been completed and the bus was on its way again. The road was dirt, with small boulders thrown in holes in the road by freighters. The bus bumped over these and even I, as a child, did not see how the bus could make any time and, particularly, better the time of the horse stages. I believe that after one trip the bus was laid up for the winter and until road conditions were more suitable."

City Incorporation

Early in 1901, the business people of Shaniko took steps to form a city government. A mayor and council had been elected at a meeting (or meetings) held in the office of the Eastern Oregon Banking Company, but the earliest record of such meetings is found in a huge leather-bound volume dated 1901-1932. Following are some gleanings from "The minutes of the first regular meeting of the Common Council of the City of Shaniko, March 16, 1901":

"Mayor F.T. Hurlburt 'in the chair' instructed the Recorder to call the roll. Present were Fen Batty, F.H. Bruner, Cooper, Lane, Lucas, and absent George Ross. A paper was read stating Rules and Procedures, and Constitutional Rights in the incorporation of the City of Shaniko. It was unanimously adopted."

The Council then set about passing the necessary ordinances concerning the operation of city government. Ross had resigned and Thomas Gavin was elected to take his place, beginning a life-long association between Gavin and City Council.

Two days later, March 18, the Council again convened, swore in Thomas Gavin, and began work on the matter of passing an ordinance to license the sale of liquor. Again, March 20, the Council met to consider issuing saloon licenses to Fen Batty for Columbia Southern Hotel bar, Julius Wiley for the saloon which opened first when Shaniko was a tent city, and F.W. Silvertooth for the saloon he was opening in Shaniko.

On April 15, 1901, the matter of sidewalks was under consideration. A bill of A.C. Sanford for "alleged work on cross walks amounting to $2 was ordered returned and corrected." It was moved that the Marshal be instructed to make necessary repairs and pick up and store at some convenient place all unused sidewalk material. In August 1902, the city ordered the finance committee to purchase lumber and place four-foot sidewalks on certain business streets, provided those most interested in such sidewalks lay the planks at their own expense. This began a project which was carried on intermittently for many years. Workmen were engaged to extend or repair the sidewalks until Shaniko had the best sidewalks for a city of its size in Central Oregon.

Also on April 15 a committee was instructed to prepare plans and submit them to contractors so they could make sealed bids on a city hall and jail to cost not less then $500 and not more than $650. The order was signed by Mayor F.T. Hurlburt. By July 1, a bid of S.B. McCarthy for $865 was referred to committee because it was not within the limits called for. A week later the Council accepted a city lot which had been offered as a gift from the Townsite Company, and the bid of McCarthy was then accepted. This building, completed on Oct. 8, 1901, "according to specifications," stands in its original location.

Perhaps some of the "wild goings-on" inspired the Council in May of 1902 to secure the services of a night watch "with a salary not to exceed $60 a month, services to cease at pleasure of Council." The special night watch was discharged with thanks for their "ever-tiring efforts" after the July 7 meeting.

On March 10, 1902, G.H. Reeder was first elected to fill the vacancy of Marshal Howell, who had sent in his resignation the week previously. (Special note might be made of the two men here mentioned as marshal, since both played significant roles in the enforcement of law for years to come. One man, Marshal Howell, at a later date, was convicted of murder of the mayor of Shaniko. The other, G.H. Reeder, continued to serve as marshal at one period or another during much of the history of Shaniko.)

There must have been some arrests during this period, for a week later a bill was presented for handcuffs and two city marshal stars, at a cost of $8.

On April 18, 1902, these notes were recorded: "Council met in Special Session for the purpose of acting upon a Health Ordinance for the City. A.C. Sanford and William Holder were elected on the Board of Health. A bill of Dr. R. Logan for $50.00 was allowed for professional services."

There were people who preferred that hogs not be allowed to roam at large in the city, for on September 7, 1903, a motion was passed to instruct the marshal to notify, in writing, all parties owning hogs to take up same and that all hogs found running at large after the 15th would be impounded and owners subject to fine. This ordinance undoubtedly related to a pigpen behind the hotel where porkers were fattened to supply meat for the dining room.

Sewers in small towns were of a primitive nature, but concern for the health of the residents led the Council to agree to furnish material for 100 lineal feet of sewer to be built by property owners and maintained by those adjacent to the line.

Portland Businessmen's Excursion Train

On May 1, 1907, the Council began to prepare for the arrival in Shaniko of a delegation of businessmen from Portland, who had investments in mind. A meeting was arranged to plan the reception for the visitors. There was a flurry of sidewalk building and a public watering trough was installed. It can only be assumed that all proceeded according to plan, since no comments were recorded as to the success of the event.

This meeting also included arrangements for more sidewalk building, including the walk to the "Owl Roost," so dubbed because a succession of bachelors (night owls?) roomed there. Later on, the band used it as a place to practice. (The site where the Owl Roost stood is the one occupied by a restaurant of Millie Pullen—later operated by Glade and Wayne McCulloch. After the restaurant closed, the place remained a Shell Station operated by Glade, until sold to Dave Gastman in 1977.)

On December 4, 1907, a committee was authorized to place sufficient street lamps, which were to be "oil lamps of good quality." After they were installed Gus Reeder was engaged to light the lamps nightly, and he did so as long as they were in use.

In March, 1908, the Council decided that all saloons be requested to close at 12 o'clock midnight and remain closed until 5 o'clock a.m. the following day. The marshal was directed to notify all saloon keepers that hereafter the ordinance prohibiting the sale of liquor on Sunday would be enforced.

Fire Bell

A special meeting for the purpose of considering purchase of a fire bell and other equipment was held on May 26, 1908. The recorder was authorized to order a 300-pound McShane fire bell, and Mr. Gavin was instructed to purchase "suitable tower for the bell and see that same is placed ready to receive bell upon its arrival." This bell is still to be seen atop its tower beside the city hall, and is still rung in case of fire.

In July of 1908, a lengthy discussion was held on ordinances. It was decided that the recorder should go to The Dalles and confer with an attorney as to the legality of the city ordinances. It would appear that abuses were causing the city fathers concern at this time, because they heard Mr. Lytle address the Council at the next meeting, requesting it to take some action on the marshal's report, and against the saloons for violation of the Sunday closing law. Mr. Lytle made it clear he was speaking for the citizens of Shaniko.

Councilman William A. Rees introduced an ordinance concerning the "licensing, regulation, and restraint of bar rooms and tippling houses and all places where liquors are sold in the City of Shaniko without a license." There followed the passing of an ordinance prohibiting the sale of intoxicating liquors to habitual drunkards, or to minors, and to make it unlawful to drink intoxicating liquors to excess.

Again the Council stressed, as it had in 1902, the illegality of "keeping, setting up, maintaining, and frequenting of houses of ill fame and houses of prostituion." Thereafter, a flurry of fines was recorded.

Assassination of the Mayor

On November 2, 1911, following the assassination of Mayor J.C. Fowlie "while on duty," the Council resolved, "That we extend to the sorrowing family and relatives our heartfelt and sincere sympathy in the hour of their grief, that the executive chair be draped in mourning for thirty days and that a copy of the resolution be sent to the family and published in the official city paper, and spread on the Official City record."

This event was a tragedy to the whole community. Mr. Fowlie was a manager of the Eastern Oregon Banking Company. He had been active in city affairs, having been councilman a number of years before being elected mayor.

On February 13, 1913, a special session was called to discuss the purchase of the City Water Works. Townsite Company agreed to $3,000 as offered, with accrued interest for the plant including the acreage containing springs and the engineer's residence. Motion made and carried.

On April 1, 1914, the Council was called to another special session to discuss the "Good Road Question," April 25 being set aside by Governor West as "Good Road Day." As a result, all available men were put to work on the roads in the city limits, the marshal to oversee the work. The men were paid 30 cents an hour.

In September of that year, applications were taken for the position as pump man. G.H. Davis was chosen from among applications of C.O. Merchant, George Dunlavey, and Davis.

In 1916, the recorder was instructed to write the district attorney for a copy of the Prohibition Law. This law was to change much of the visible habits of the drinking public. Saloons were closed, and any sales of liquor had to be "under the counter" if at all.

The proceedings reflected the events occurring in the First World War years,. Mr. Burkhead, school principal, suggested the city fly a United States flag over the City Hall, and a committee was appointed to purchase "same." There was a great turn-over in council membership as men moved, enlisted, or came to town to take the place of those leaving.

January 5, 1932, was the last posted meeting in this book of council proceedings.

MAYORS OF SHANIKO

1901	F.T. Hurlburt
1904	E.O. Woodbury
1907	W.E. Lytle
1908	D.M. McLauchlan (must have resigned)
1909	J.C. Fowlie (installed January 6, 1909; assassinated February, 1912)
1912	W.A. Rees appointed to finish J.C. Fowlie's term.
1915-1926	Tom Gavin
1932-1937	Tom Gavin
1938	Wayne McCulloch
1940	W.A. Rees
1942-1952	Frank Wagner
1953-1955	Gerald Johnson
1957	Beck Whitesell appointed
1958	Ruby Hester—term completed by John Reeder.
1960	John Reeder until July 1—Joe Morelli sworn in.
1963	Frank Gatsinger. Resigned in October. Helen Sands appointed. Resigned in July, 1964. Tom Jordan appointed. In November 1964, he moved and Dave Wilson was appointed.
1965	Ralph Jacobs
1967	Dave Wilson
1969	Pat Shay
1971	Vergil Steinmetz
1972	August—Bob Bawlby
1973	Sue Morelli "acting"
1975	Ruth Lang
1977	Jim Oakes
	Julia Robinson appointed
	Dave Gastman

5

FIRST PEOPLE OF SHANIKO

Elmer Lytle

Elmer Lytle, who was railroad station agent at The Dalles, was one of the first persons to conceive the idea of building a railroad through Sherman County. He was a signatory of the incorporation papers for the Columbia Southern Railway Company in 1897.

He was born in Pennsylvania in 1861, then when grown, became a telegrapher. From 1880 until 1897 he was agent for the Oregon Washington Railroad & Navigation Company at Waitsburg, Washington.

After the rails reached Shaniko, Mr. Lytle is mentioned several times in the City Council records. In March 1903, an ordinance was passed granting him the right-of-way to build a railway through certain streets and alleyways of the city. At that time there was some thought of extending the Columbia Southern Line south to Madras. Permission was given "provided Mr. Lytle shall within two years have actually constructed and equipped five miles of the proposed railroad." The extension was deemed impractical because of deep canyons and steep grades south of Shaniko, so the plan was abondoned.

Mr. Lytle was elected in 1906 to fill the unexpired term of Mayor Hurlburt. He was not afraid to speak out about illegal practices in the saloons in Shaniko and took action to curb the lawlessness of the early years. He brought one of the saloon keepers before the Council in October 1907 to confer with members for the purpose of devising means to abate nuisances reported to exist in his saloon.

About 1908, Elmer Lytle went on to further railroad construction. He was involved in the building of the P.R. & N. (Portland Railroad & Navigation) line from Hillsboro to Tillamook.

Gustav Henry Reeder

While the commerce of the so-called "Wool Capital of the World" was developing, the people who kept the gears well oiled and the harness repaired, the warehouses operating, and the home fires burning were setting down their roots in the rocky soil of Shaniko. Gus Reeder was one of them.

Gustav Henry "Gus" Rehder, long-time marshal of Shaniko, was born in Wheatland, Clinton County, Iowa, January 23, 1868. For over 50 years Gus Reeder was a vital part of the affairs of Shaniko. From the time he arrived in 1889 until his wife, Wilhelmina Burr, died in 1951, Gus was Shaniko's "Jack of All Trades."

His brother, Joshua Michael "Mike," came to Oregon first in 1885, then sent for Gus to join him. When Gus arrived in 1889, he learned that his brother had changed the spelling of the family name of Rehder to Reeder. Thereafter, they were partners in the stock-raising business under the name of Reeder Bros.

In 1906, Gus opened shop as a harness and saddle-maker, one of Shaniko's earliest businesses. His place was destroyed by the big fire of 1911. He began business again in a smaller shop adjacent to the Columbia Southern Hotel. Here he did leather work and repaired and sold shoes. Eventually the use of cars and trucks ended the harness repair business but he continued to do minor leather work and shoe repairs, along with his other activities, until he closed the shop and retired in 1950.

Gus Reeder helped build the school house, spent many hours employed as city marshal, was stock brand inspector for the area, and during Prohibition was deputy sheriff of Southern Wasco County under Levi Chrisman. He was always active in city affairs. In 1909, and again in 1917, he was elected as pump man for the City Water Works. In 1919, the Reeders moved to the city-owned house at Cross Hollows. (After the Cross Hollows Inn burned perhaps in 1917, date not known, a new house had been built to house the water maintenance engineer.)

Gus remained pump man, repairing and—in winter— thawing out broken mains. It became difficult in later years to keep the old and leaking pipes usable. In addition to all his other duties, Gus served as clerk on the school board for many years.

Reeder never moved from Cross Hollows until after Mrs. Reeder died. Then he went to Moro to live with his daughter, Elsie Jones, and her husband, Tommy.

Since Gus was "Mr. Shaniko" in so many capacities, different people had their own memories of him: "He was a friendly man, but some people were a little in awe of him, maybe because he represented the law." "I remember him lighting the street lamps in all kinds of weather—like The Old Lamplighter." "He worked at his cobbler's bench, cobbler's nails in one side of his mouth and his old, crooked-stemmed pipe in the other. Somehow, he still managed to tell stories about the early days even while he went on working." Others remember his shop and the smell of leather, shoe polish and dust that met them at the door.

Gus had a strong sense of responsibility concerning his position as marshal. Long after Prohibition ended and beer was legalized, he would stop at Glade's Shell Station on his water-rent collecting rounds, with his marshal's badge pinned to his vest. Before ordering, he would unpin his badge and tuck it in his pocket out of sight while he drank his glass of beer.

It was Gus Reeder's custom to lock up his shop and go to the depot at train time to wait with others for the arrival of the train. In this picture taken about 1908, a group are already on hand. *Left to right are:* W.A. Rees and son Harry, Bill Wornstaff, two unidentified men, and on the extreme right, a man named Lamborn.

When asked why his mustache was so black when his hair was so gray, he responded, "Because my mustache is 20 years younger than my hair." It was his custom to lock up shop and go to the depot at train time, then follow the mail to the post office to "pass the time of day" with people there until the mail was 'put out.'

It was in 1900 that he married Wilhelmina Burr, a young girl who at that time was working at Cross Hollows Station for the Gus Schmidt family. Wilhelmina was born in Shingletown, California, in 1880, a daughter of Adison and Mary Burr. The family moved to Days Creek, Oregon, and then to Antelope. Gus and Wilhelmina were the first couple to be married in Shaniko. (April 30). They celebrated their Golden Wedding Anniversary at Shaniko Hotel in 1950.

The first few years of their marriage they lived in a small house Gus built just south of the water tower. Wilhelmina, a hard-working young woman, was soon baking bread to sell. Years later she had large boxes of bread shipped up on the train from The Dalles to meet the needs of her customers.

After they moved to Cross Hollows, the work load increased for her, adding gardening, care of the milk they

Thomas Gavin came on the first train that arrived in Shaniko, to manage Pease & Mays Department Store. He attended the first City council meeting, and served on the council continuously as councilman or mayor for 35 years.

were selling in town, as well as looking after their growing family. Through it all, Mrs. Reeder lived up to the teachings of her faith in the Christian Science Church. She died in March 31, 1951, and Gus followed her, August 22, 1956.

Thomas Gavin

Thomas Gavin was on the first train that arrived in Shaniko, sent there by Pease & Mays Department Store in The Dalles, to manage their branch store in the new city. He continued in charge of the store until 1919, when he and Roy R. Wheeler bought it from Edward C. Pease Company. (Roy Wheeler sold out his interest in what became "Gavin-Wheeler Company" at the end of 1929.)

About ten weeks before Gavin and Wheeler purchased the store, Ivan Olsen started work as the delivery boy, age 11 years. He continued to work in the store until Mr. Gavin's death, when he purchased the entire holdings of the company.

Thomas Gavin was born on a farm near Rockbridge, Greene County, Illinois, March 30, 1866. He was educated in the ten-grade school at Kone, about fifteen miles from his birthplace. During the years 1887-8, he attended the Valparaiso, Indiana, Normal School and graduated from the commercial department. In 1888, he arrived in Portland to work for J.N. Bristol in his Morrison Street grocery store. In 1899, he went to The Dalles where he worked in the grocery department of the Pease and Mays Company store. Gavin attended the first City council meeting in Shaniko and served on the City Council continuously, first as councilman, then as mayor, until just before his death in 1936. His first term of office as mayor was 1915-1926, then again from 1932-1936.

POSTMASTERS OF SHANIKO, MARCH 31, 1900—AUGUST 8, 1981

March 31, 1900	John Wilcox
Nov. 1, 1900	William Holder
Oct. 20,1902	Alfred Sanford
Feb. 21, 1906	Archibald McCully
April 26, 1910	John Coe
Oct. 14, 1913	Leola Loring
May 10, 1918	Ruth Bogart
April 1, 1925	Richard Kinney
Nov. 1, 1946	Maude Garrett
July 1, 1957	Mary A. Hanks
Sept. 9, 1966	Alice Roberts
Jan. 26, 1980	Elizabeth R. Spires
Aug. 8, 1981	Cora Willich

Shaniko Post Offices

There is a likelihood that mail was delivered very early from the Columbia Southern Hotel, though that is hard to verify. John D. Wilcox was the first postmaster, and William Holder followed him. Since Holder was publisher of the *Shaniko Leader*, it is to be assumed that the post office was in his shop. We know that Alfred C. Sanford, the next post-master, maintained the office in his store, just south of the brick hotel.

Sanford's daughter recalled that when her father had the Shaniko post office it handled the third highest volume of mail west of the Mississippi River. The postal area covered 2800 square miles. Trucks drawn by Percheron horses met the incoming train, loaded the mail sacks and brought them to the post office behind the store. When the mail was sort-ed, stage coaches picked up their assignment of mail and pas-sengers and started out for their destinations.

When Archibald D. McCully became postmaster, the office was in the back of Pease & Mays store, where it stayed until after John H. Coe turned it over to Leola Loring, who moved the boxes to the building that first housed Sanford's store. She kept the telephone switchboard also. The post office remained there while Ruth Bogart and Richard Kinney were in charge. Kinney remodeled the building. He held the position of postmaster longer than anyone before or since. He was in charge from April 1, 1925, until his retirement in November 1946. His wife, Ethel Kinney, was telephone operator. When the Kinneys left, the telephone switchboard was removed.

Maude Garrett maintained the office where it was, but when Pat Hanks was appointed, her husband Bill moved the building west to the former Pease & Mays location, and it became Pat & Bill's service station and post office. Pat was postmaster until Alice Roberts took her place in 1966.

Ed Martin built a new office in 1972 on the site of the old Sanford store where Shaniko Post Office had stood so many years. The furnishings were moved back from the service station and Shaniko Post Office was "home again."

Gustav Schmidt

Gustav Schmidt, a German homesteader near Cross Hol-lows, bought the stage station inn at Cross Hollows from Farr when he moved to Antelope. Schmidt used the first Scherneckau store building for a woodshed and bunk house.

Gus had come to Cross Hollows in 1887 and bought sheep to graze on the hills. As happened to other stockmen, he lost most of his first band of sheep during the heavy winter of 1889-90. When he recovered from this set-back, he went to Germany and brought back Antonia Eastkraut as his wife. She spoke no English but gradually learned from the children living nearby.

An Indian family lived down the canyon below Cross Hollows. The man was blind. The woman came and did washing for Antonia. Other Indians came every spring to camp in the canyon where they skinned dead sheep, gathered tufts of wool hanging from barbed-wire fences, and picked wild berries. About two miles below the Indian residence near Pine Hollow there was an Indian burial ground. Gus had a sheep camp there.

There were two small meadows at Cross Hollows, one at the house and one along the creek on the way to the big spring about 15 to 25 yards below the upper one. It was near the lower meadow that the spring was boarded up to collect water for the big storage basin furnishing water for the City of Shaniko.

A man was buried at Cross Hollows while the Schmidts lived there. In a drunken condition, he fell over a wagon tongue. They carried him into the house but he was dead.

Members of the Schmidt family lived in the general area for many years.

Governor Zenas Ferry Moody

Former Governor Zenas Ferry Moody was a man of many interests and boundless activities, only one of which was operating the Moody Warehouse Company in The Dalles. In 1900, he saw Shaniko as a good place to expand his business, and by 1902, the new warehouse he built there was open and ready to do business. When Zenas Moody realized that better prices could be offered the sheep and cattlemen of Central Oregon if the California wool buyers had more competition, he invited Boston firms to send bidders to the sales that were attracting attention—not only because of the great quantity of wool coming in, but because of the high quality of the fibres as well. Thus Central Oregon ranchers benefited from his business acumen.

Zenas Moody sent his son, William H. Moody to manage the new warehouse. At first Bill Moody lived at the Columbia Southern Hotel. As soon as there was a house available, he moved in and invited Bill Rees and his bride, Lillie, to live with him. Mrs. Moody and their son, Adelbert, and daughter, Drusilla, were still living in The Dalles during the school year. In the summer, the two families lived together in the two-bedroom house and Adelbert helped his father in the warehouse. After the Rees house was built and the Moody children had finished high school, Clara Moody closed their home in The Dalles and made Shaniko the permanent home of the Moody family.

It was possible to live the good life in Shaniko, and the Moodys did. A telephone call in the afternoon assured delivery the next day of any special foods they wanted—even such luxuries of the day as a gunnysack of fresh oysters from the coast, dried fruits, or large cans of fresh maple syrup from Vermont. To chill the fresh fruits and produce, 100-pound blocks of ice, packed in sawdust, were delivered by train. (Mrs. Moody was a fabulous cook.)

When the warehouse crew rose early in the morning to load out stock, Clara Moody spent the time baking doughnuts which she sent to the warehouse along with a huge, blue-enameled pot of coffee made with fresh-ground beans, as a mid-morning refreshment for the workers.

The Moodys traveled a good deal for the times in which they lived, going to Lake Tahoe, Lake Chelan, and to Alaska. Bill Rees managed the warehouse when they were away.

Bill and Clara Moody. The Moodys lived the good life in Shaniko. A telephone call to The Dalles or Portland one morning usually ensured the arrival the following day of fresh oysters from the coast, maple syrup from Jones Cash Store in Portland, or a hundred-pound block of ice from The Dalles.

A string of wagons loaded with the mammoth sacks of wool waits to unload at the Moody Warehouse.

About 1914, Bill Moody was felled by a severe stroke which made it impossible for him to return to the warehouse. The Moodys had kept a cook for several years. Katy Estebennet lived in a small house they had built for her in the back yard. Now it became necessary to keep a nurse, as well, to assist with Mr. Moody's care. In 1919 Bill Moody died.

In a year or two, Clara Moody sold the warehouses to Bill Rees, but she maintained her home in Shaniko. She was again free to travel and to visit relatives in The Dalles, Portland and California. Much of the social life in Shaniko centered around the periods when Mrs. Moody was at home.

During the Depression the investments Mrs. Moody had made in Portland failed and she began taking roomers. At different times during the next few years those who lived in her home were C.L. Coffey, Mrs. Mayfield, Virginia Cram, and Maude Joynt. One night in 1933, Clara Moody quietly died in her sleep. She was buried beside her husband in the Odd Fellows Cemetery in The Dalles.

William Arthur Rees

A Welsh immigrant, William Arthur Rees was first seen in Shaniko in 1900. He was sent by the Moody Warehouse Company in The Dalles to "advance money to teamsters and others on consignments of wool, with headquarters at the Railroad Depot (space in front of the Shaniko Warehouse). The following year he returned, to become a permanent resident and bookkeeper for the new warehouse under construction by Zenas Moody. Like most single businessmen, he lived at the Columbia Southern Hotel. It was there that he met and courted Lillie McHargue, niece of James Keeney who managed that brick hotel. Lillie was head waitress in the spacious dining room. Her father, James McHargue, operated the nearby Hotel Shaniko (not Shaniko Hotel). Her grandfather James K. McHargue and family had crossed

William A. Rees and bride Lillie McHargue. Bill Rees, an immigrant from Wales, was first seen in Shaniko in 1900, sent by Moody Warehouse Company of The Dalles to advance money to teamsters on consignments of wool. He lived at the Columbia Southern Hotel, and it was there that he met and courted Lillie McHargue, niece of James Keeney, manager of the hotel.

The Reeses built their own home in 1907. *Left to right:* Son Harry, Lillie and Adelbert. Picture taken in about 1909. The Rees home faces the warehouse on the corner of 5th and F streets.

For 67 years Lillie **Rees** lived a life of quiet service in the town of Shaniko. She died just a few days before her 93rd birthday. At her funeral in The Dalles, The Rev. John Richardson read the following passage from the Bible: "A wife of a noble character, who can find, she is worth more than rubies; She selects wool and flax and works with eager hands." Lillie was engaged in such good works in 1964 when this picture was taken.

the plains with the Brown party who settled Brownsville, Oregon, in 1846.

After their marriage, the Rees couple lived in one of the few available houses. Bill Moody had rented the house so his family could join him in Shaniko during summer vacations. The Reeses built their own home in 1907.

Bill Rees worked for Moody Company in Shaniko until after Moody died. Eventually he bought the warehouses from Moody's widow. He remained in the warehouse business until retirement in 1942. The couple made their home in Shaniko the rest of their lives. He died in May 1955.

For 67 years Lillie lived a life of quiet service in the town of Shaniko. She gave generously to friends and neighbors the produce from her garden and the fruits of her labors in the kitchen, the fragrance of baked rolls wafted in the air, as though she were running a bakery.

For many years the nearest doctor was at The Dalles, 75 miles away. Mrs. Rees had a store of practical pioneer knowledge, so she was often called upon to administer first aid, or give minor medical advice. Her well-stocked basket of bandages and ointments was ready for emergency calls. In at least two instances she laid out the dead for burial.

If there was dissension in town, she was the first to make overtures as a peacemaker. When some community project was under way, she could be found helping. The Rees home was a haven of rest and comfort for weary travelers, be they bishops, clergy, school teachers, or health nurses traveling through, or in town on business.

Mrs. Rees died in March 1968, a month short of her 93rd birthday.

6

SCHOOLS AND CHURCH

Shaniko School

Details of the first school classes held in Shaniko are only known in part, and that through the memory of Agnes Schmidt (Hinkle). Mrs. Hinkle remembers that the parents paid Miss Smith, (by subscription) to teach one term at least. The date is not known.

Mrs. Rojinia Campbell Hunt, in her later years, recounted her firsthand experience of teaching a three months' summer session in Shaniko, in a story written by Mrs. Raymond Crabtree about 1952:

Memories of Mrs. Hunt

"When I arrived in Shaniko practically everyone was living in tents drawn over board frames. Several business houses, however, had already been built—A.C. Sanford's Cash Grocery, Bolton's General Merchandise, Pease and Mays' five-unit department store, restaurants, several saloons and a recreation hall. A newspaper, *The Shaniko Leader*, was in a building of its own, too, and the city water reservoir was in use.

"That fall when I left for home, the new depot was completed, the bank vault, and several long sheds so that the sheep could be brought into town for spring shearing.

"But to get to the school—a building had been hurriedly thrown together just prior to my arrival. Made of green lumber, not battened, there were cracks between the boards

nearly an inch wide. I remember that Mr. Al Esping came in the first morning with three pieces of thin wooden material something like plywood, which he nailed to the wall and painted for our blackboards. The desks and seats were home-made and my own desk was a pulpit since the building was to be used also as a church.

"Twenty-eight students enrolled that summer. We had an average attendance of twenty-three. After I had each child graded and placed, we had every grade except the seventh. One girl rode horseback eight miles each morning. She was eighteen years old, but never before had had an opportunity to go to school. She was really studious and by my giving her extra time and by her own hard work she was able to begin with the fourth grade. I was really proud of her before the summer was over.

"We had the regular subjects for the grade school of that day. Also I ran quite a kindergarten. Since there were no regulations, the mothers sent four- and five-year-olds to school just to get the youngsters off the street and out from under the horses' hooves.

"And in addition to the children, at least a dozen dogs came regularly every day with their respective masters and departed only when their masters were dismissed. It did no good to put them out and shut the door because they just put their noses to the cracks and whined so no one could study. Besides, we couldn't stand having the door closed. During the entire day those dogs lay panting along the side of the room, adding immeasurably to the heat. They were good natured though, and we had very few dog fights.

"I used a hand bell as teachers did in those days, and it was no time at all before the dogs listened for the bell and did everything right along with the children. Dismissal got to be called 'the circus' and townspeople occasionally stood outside just to watch. But I had good order; the children liked it better that way and I did too!

"Mr. Sanford was made chairman of the school board. The other two members of the board were Mr. M.L. Lane, the village blacksmith, and Mr. H. Brunner. The school clerk, Dr. Ray Logan, was nearly worked to death that summer with so many cases of typhoid fever.

"Salary? Well, as I said, it was a subscription school, but I received $45 a month and $15 of that went for board. The plan was for the teacher to 'board around' staying two weeks with a family, but in Shaniko very few families had homes. Even at the end of the summer there were only six residences. Mrs. Sanford was willing, so I just continued to board with her, but I shared my bed with two other young women, and our room was very small. It was difficult but not so impossible as a one-family tent.

"It was September 20th when I started home. That was Saturday. On the following Thursday I took the boat at The Dalles for Portland, and came face to face with Dr. Logan. We were surprised, and I couldn't imagine why he should be taking the much slower boat instead of the train. Then he told me.

"On Tuesday, a whole block of the business section of Shaniko had burned. His office had been in one section of the large building owned by Pease & Mays and he, with others, had lost everything they possessed. The reservoir had been full of water but with no fire-fighting equipment, the men had been powerless.

"Years later, Genevieve, our daughter, insisted she must go to Shaniko where her mother had been instrumental in forming the school district. She graduated from there in 1924 when Clyde T. Bonney was principal.

A Child's Theme

Occasionally a piece of paper, with school work brought home by a child, remains intact, giving an idea of the work being accomplished. On September 8, 1913, nine-year-old Adelbert Rees wrote the following history of Shaniko in a neat, clear script:

"Shaniko is a little village in Oregon. There are two stores, one restaurant, one blacksmith shop, one butcher shop, two warehouses, one depot, one round house, one school house, three saloons and one barley roll. It grinds wheat, oats, and barley, and there are 27 families. There is a main street. The mud is about ten yards deep. There were two cases of scarlet fever in town. One was Bleakneys and one was Mallets."

Shaniko High School, 1918

Grade school was a regular part of town life in Shaniko after the establishment of the school district, as described by

Mrs. Hunt, but it was nearly 15 years before there was a high school. The first class to graduate (1921) consisted of three students, Ray Logan, Alice Olsen, and Adelbert Rees. The following year only two graduates received diplomas.

In 1924, Clyde T. Bonney became principal of the Shaniko School. During the years he taught there he brought students from Maupin, Tygh Valley, and Clarno to live in town during the week and attend high school classes. This swelled the ranks of students for two or three years before other arrangements were made for these out-of-town students. The last class to graduate consisted of Marguerite Reeder and Phyllis Hanna, in 1934.

The high school was never attended by more than a handful of students. Maintaining school in so small a community was not easy, but did enable the parents to have close ties with faculty and school. The most obvious lack was in courses offered. Some students took post-graduate courses in The Dalles before entering college.

Episcopal Church

The first recorded visit of an Episcopal clergyman to Shaniko and Antelope was mentioned in the diary of Bishop Benjamin Wistar Morris, then bishop of all of Oregon, who tells about going in 1875 from Canyon City to Burns, Prineville, Shaniko (Scherneckau's) and then to The Dalles. By 1907, the State of Oregon had been separated into two areas, the diocese of Oregon and the Missionary District of Eastern Oregon, with the Rt. Rev. R.L. Paddock appointed the first acting bishop of all Oregon east of the Cascades.

The New York *Journal* carried the following article in 1899: "The policy of sensational methods to attract young people to the church, which has gone as far as dancing in several places, went a step farther last night in the Protestant Episcopal Pro-Cathedral. Boxing matches and a wrestling bout were introduced with the approval of the authorities

Mr. and Mrs. Clyde T. Bonney. In 1924 Mr. Bonney became principal of the Shaniko school. During the years he taught there he brought students from Maupin, Tygh Valley, and Clarno to attend high school.

Shaniko High School while Clyde Bonney was Principal. *First row from left: standing*, Edna Gott, Irma Hoech, Margaret Rees, Edith Hanna, Alma Hall, Faye New Geneviene Hunt, Gertie Doering. *Second Row:* Shultis Slyter, Fred Miller, Ivan Olsen, Mr. Bonney, Clifford Brown, Willis Brittain, Thelma Bonney, Crystal Wagonblast, *Back Row:* Harry Rees, Clifford McCorkle, Clifford Miller, Clarence Nelson, Frank Fisk, Henry McGreer.

and under the eye of the Rev. Mr. Paddock, the vicar, who seemed to enjoy them. They had the grace to quote the vicar's stated motive—to keep young men's interest and keep them off the streets and the worst places which abound in all the neighborhood.

"In 1900, his collar offered the Rev. Paddock little protection from solicitation on the streets as he worked to find ways to help women and children. He was able to get a Resolution for Investigation into the Episcopal convention in 1900, and for the first time the church became involved in the moral issues of politics and sex."

When ordained bishop of Eastern Oregon in December, 1907, Robert Paddock had just returned from a year of travel in the Holy Land. He and his wife left immediately for Oregon. They visited her sister in San Francisco, en route. While there Mrs. Paddock became desperately ill and died, leaving the bishop with two daughters and an assignment that would have staggered a lesser man. He decided to leave the girls with Mrs. Paddock's sister in San Francisco and go on to Central Oregon alone.

The work of Bishop Paddock was, presumably, to establish a church in each community where the faithful could worship. In those days missionary societies were actively financing the establishment of churches in new communities in the West. In 1908, Eastern Oregon was the most rural and least populated frontier of America. Bishop Paddock came to men who lived with sheep and cattle, mines and timber.

There were several families of Anglicans in Shaniko and Antelope—among them, the Reeses in Shaniko and the Boltons and Roopers in Antelope. Mrs. William A. Rees tells of one visit, not unique, when the Bishop rented a horse and rode out to Antelope for services, eight miles away, in a freezing white fog. He arrived cold and miserable, and built a fire in the chill of the church. After the service he went to a parishioner's home for the night. The guest room, called "The Bishop's House," was apart from the house and without heat. There he shivered and tried to sleep, but in the early morning he was up and rode the horse back in the cold fog to Shaniko. At the Rees home he accepted a cup of hot tea and drank it standing behind the coal stove next to the warm wall, then rushed to the depot a block away to catch the train.

Once, a mulligan supper was planned on Friday night, to be held in the depot, so Bishop Paddock might become better acquainted with the men of the community. Church services were held later at the schoolhouse. Several people were confirmed. "A large crowd attended," according to a *Maupin Times* clipping dated 1918.

Across from the Columbia Southern Hotel a platform was being used for a dance floor (probably the floor of a building under construction.) When Bishop Paddock arrived in Shaniko, he went into the saloons, greeting people and asking them to bring lanterns and stools to the service he planned to hold outside. The bishop was known to be a dynamic speaker. The saloons closed, and the platform was filled at the appointed hour. He didn't mind asking Methodist, Catholic, or other congregations for permission to hold services in their church buildings. Most of his time was spent traveling to ranches and farms miles from town, to find the scattered members of the flock.

Perhaps because of the unorthodox manner of the bishop's approach, and his failure to build church buildings, he came under scrutiny of the National Episcopal Church. But he was undaunted by the conflict, being too busy traveling and preaching in out-of-the-way places to give it more than a passing thought.

Bishop Paddock was not a methodical man where accounts were concerned, and often he just stuffed offerings into his topcoat pocket and emptied the contents on his desk when he reached Hood River, the Diocesan Center. Altar Guilds in The Dalles and some of the larger towns complained that he appeared at services with mud on his boots.

There were rumors and gossip. Finally he was recalled to New York to answer to the governing bishops.

He was charged with disloyalty. Eventually, the strain of overwork, followed by his recall, brought about a nervous collapse.

A member of the Bishop's Committee in Hood River defended Bishop Paddock by saying, "He has been the life of the Church in our district, and he has been performing a great work in Eastern Oregon, and we resent these charges, so obviously trivial." Speaking of the charges of disloyalty to the Episcopal Church made against Bishop Paddock, Dr. W.A. Smith, editor of *The Churchman*, said, "He has worked in a hard, rough country, where the Church sent him to convert men to Christ, and much of that time he has to travel in Khaki, with blankets on his back, yet he has been criticized for not always carrying his bishop's robes on his journeys."

Bishop Paddock recovered and lived the rest of his life in the East.

7

CAPTURED IN MEMORY

Harry E. Hill

Harry E. Hill was born at The Dalles, March 9, 1892. His vivid memories of living in Shaniko during the years 1900 to 1905 open up the past as viewed through the eyes of an alert, intensely active child. He was involved in almost every aspect of community life open to a youngster. Little seems to have escaped his notice, or faded from his memory. His story agrees remarkably well with historical data already prepared for this book. It has been helpful in rounding out details of events.

Mr. Hill now lives in a retirement community in Eugene, Oregon. There is little indication of change in his nature. The gray in his hair and his age authenticate his story of participation in Shaniko affairs of 1900, but the spring in his step and his interest in people around him reveal that he is still the same Harry at heart.

Recollections of Harry Hill

"My father was The Dalles agent for Pacific Express Company at the time Elmer Lytle was railroad station agent at The Dalles. The two families lived a block apart and knew each other well. This was before Elmer Lytle conceived the idea of building a railroad from Biggs to Shaniko. After the project was carried through and the Shaniko Warehouse Company was hiring men, my father, Frank N. Hill, became bookkeeper, probably influenced by Mr. Lytle.

"We took the train from The Dalles to Biggs, and there transferred to the Columbia Southern rail line. The train had a grade to climb most of the way and when we reached Kent, water for the engine was exhausted. The engine was disconnected from the rest of the train and ran into Shaniko where it got a supply of water, returned to the train, hooked up and went on into Shaniko. I was eight years of age and did not think or know of the reason for delay, but later learned that this method of handling was a regular occurrence, since Kent always had a water shortage.

"When we arrived at the Shaniko station, snow was on the ground and some flakes were in the air. It was some time in the early winter of 1900. My father met us and took us to the Columbia Southern Hotel. Hotel Shaniko was down the street a block. A rooming house and hotel were built later, across the corner from it, and operated by a Chinese man. The only other Chinese in town were those in a house across the tracks where clothing was laundered. Some of us boys were sent there occasionally to pick up or leave laundry. We were fascinated by the pig-tailed Chinamen filling their mouths with water, then spitting or spraying it on the clothes they were ironing.

"When I was about twelve years old, a representative of the Troy Laundry of Portland came to Shaniko and somehow I became involved as the Shaniko agent for the Troy Laundry. My time was already well occupied with school, carrying the papers, and working in the store on week-ends and after school, but I was instructed in the mechanics of laundry salesmanship by the Troy man and furnished a large basket which was to be shipped to Portland when filled with soiled clothing. Then the Troy representative left town.

"I was in competition with the Chinese laundry, but didn't know it. I must have had that agency for two months when it was abruptly cancelled by the smallpox epidemic. A drummer from Pennsylvania came down with smallpox, which immediately spread over town. The hotel where the drummer was staying was quarantined, and so were many homes in town.

"A hostler named Morgan, at·Del Howell's livery stable, had given me some laundry to be done and I had included it in the basket for Portland. When the basket was returned, a shirt was missing, and Mr. Morgan confronted me each evening when I delivered the paper, demanding his shirt back. However, he had put a blanket on his bunk which the ailing drummer had used, with the result that Mr. Morgan died of smallpox. Obviously, I was never bothered by Mr. Morgan about his shirt after that, but my laundry business fizzled.

"Dr. Perkins, who resided in Shaniko and had an office and drugstore there, first was called to the hotel when the drummer became ill, and apparently an *Oregonian* editorial criticized the doctor for not having made a proper diagnosis. The doctor was one of my customers, and as a result of the editorial, I lost his trade—he left town.

"I don't remember the number of people who died; persons placed the figure at fifty. That looks a little high, but perhaps it was so. The bodies were disposed of by putting the boxes on sledges and dragging the latter by horses around the town rather than through it. The sledges went by at night and could not be seen by us, although we could plainly hear the noise as they were drawn over the rough ground. Burial was in a ravine east of the railroad. Rocks were piled and strewn over the graves to prevent digging by animals.

"Later, some of us boys were down that way and discovered several piles of Indian arrowheads which apparently had been placed there by previous inhabitants years before. As boys do, we kicked the piles apart and used the arrowheads as rocks to throw at nearby objects. Some years later I told a friend of mine about the arrowheads and described the location; he made a special trip from Portland but was unable to find any.

Sheep shearing at the Rooper ranch. At shearing time in the spring there was an influx of shearers; most of them brought their own hand-operated clippers. (Old Wasco County Pioneers Association picture.)

"King Lytle, whose father Charles was depot agent, was given a pony of his own, incurring the envy of the rest of us boys by riding up and down Shaniko's main street. He kept the horse at Del Howell's stables for $15 a month—which the other town boys could not afford. However, Del was willing to let us ride his horses to exercise them. Some of the boys got horses as colts at the annual round-up of wild horses. Country boys of the vicinity had their own horses.

"Just outside town, on the west end, were the sheep-shearing pens and holding yards for sheep to be shipped out by rail within the next day or two. At sheep-shearing time in the spring there would be an influx of shearers; most would have their own clippers. Each shearer would be assigned his own small pen and a sheep would be herded into it; the shearer would grab the sheep and start clipping. Often a man would visit the various pens carrying a jug of whiskey and a small glass. This source of stimulation would be offered each man and, in most cases, accepted. When one sheep was sheared, it would be herded away and replaced by another.

"Next would be the trip to the dipping vats in the canyon east of Cross Hollows, where the sheep were dipped for scabies. The vats of sheep dip were just deep and wide enough to accommodate the sheep as it was pushed forward by attendants with long poles, but narrow enough to prevent the animal from turning around. As the sheep proceeded the length of the vat, the attendant would push the head of the animal under the liquid to assure that is penetrated all parts of the sheep's skin.

"After this, the sheep would be herded out onto the open range again. There were usually several bands of sheep in the area near Shaniko, each attended by one or more herders. Each herder had several working sheep dogs to help him keep away the coyotes and move the sheep.

"Wild horses were numerous in the area. It was thrilling to see an alarmed band of horses streaming by, the leader with his head high and tail straight to the rear, running into the distance. The horses were brought to the railroad corrals at Shaniko and culled, the good ones being retained for use and the balance shipped to Portland. probably for glue.

"This was the time when the boys could get colts. From a financial standpoint, the colts seemed to have little value. This was true, too, of colts born to freight-wagon horses. I have seen a team standing still off the road while a mare brought a foal into the world. The freighter then would take a hammer and hit the colt in the forehead to kill it, wait an hour or more, put the mare back into harness and drive off, leaving the body of the newborn colt to the coyotes.

"There were freighters who came into town in a hook-up of three or four wagons, pulled by four-or six-horse teams, depending on the season and road conditions. At wool time the wagons were loaded with great bags of wool which would be baled at the Shaniko Warehouse. The empty wagons and teams were housed overnight at the wagon yard, an enclosed space located down near the 'Houses of Pleasure' run by Lil Hamilton.

"Lil was the only woman in town who smoked cigarettes openly. Sometimes she would come in the back door and signal me to sell her some cigarettes, which, of course, I did.

She was one of my *Oregonian* customers. She also was an object of aversion in town should the ladies encounter her.

"Impromptu horse races were common and usually developed from heated arguments between horse owners in a local bar. They assembled a short distance west of town, made their bets, and put their horses to the test. They were usually accompanied by men and boys (including me) who were footloose and wanted some excitement. When the races were run and the bets paid, the crowd dispersed—but I often stayed on to watch the prairie dogs stand tall in front of their holes until some movement caused them to drop down out of sight. These gopher holes could be hazardous to a horse that inadvertently stepped into one. A broken leg was often the horse's fate.

"Rattlesnakes were numerous, not so much on the plateau on which the town stood, as in the surrounding canyons. I recall riding bareback on an old white horse in the canyon east of Cross Hollows, to get our cow. Suddenly the horse shied and backed up. I went over her shoulder and landed in the dirt of the road. The rattler was coiled in front of me. Instinctively I started rolling and did so until I was out of striking distance and the snake had slithered out of sight.

"In the spring, after the snow had melted and the rains came, ponds formed. Soon the area around the pond was a mass of buttercups, like great yellow blankets. Frogs appeared and at night their croaks could be heard for miles in the still air.

"Some moonlight nights when the snow was on the ground, we would hear the coyotes howl and see them sitting on their haunches in a semi-circle, always far enough away so that they could not be reached by the shots fired from my twenty-two.

"Baseball was the most popular sport. The ball diamond and bleachers were located east of the tracks. A men's team sent a challenge to neighboring towns, such as Wasco, Moro, and Grass Valley. At the railroad roundhouse there was usually a spare locomotive standing as a back-up for the engine on the regular run from Biggs. In times of high baseball fever, enthusiasts would prevail upon the railroad officials to run a special train carrying baseball teams and fans to one of the other towns. On the way, there was excitement with heavy betting and much liquid stimulation. The return to Shaniko would be enthusiastic or not, according to the fortunes of the Shaniko team. Sometimes the train brought teams and visitors from other towns to Shaniko to play.

"All this changed, however, with advent of the smallpox epidemic in 1903, when long rows of sheds were built on the baseball grounds to house patients, mostly transients, and their attendants.

Following is an account from the *Oregonian*, Aug. 7, 1960, of one of these early ball games, written by Walter F. Perry of Moro.

Shaniko Ball Game

"To The Editor: You have printed a couple of articles about Shaniko when it was a boom town, and I am reminded of a baseball game that I saw there in the summer of 1901 between Wasco and Shaniko to decide who was the champion of Eastern Oregon.

"Wasco always had a good team, and Shaniko thought they could have a good team too, from the large number of young men that had come up there to work in the wool shipping center, the largest in the world. So they sent a challenge to Wasco, and also informed them that they would have several thousand dollars to bet on the game. Wasco accepted the challenge, and made arrangements with the Columbia Southern Railroad to haul them out the following Sunday.

"Well, the railroad did haul a large train load of people, stopping at Wasco, Moro and Grass Valley to pick up passengers. We got the surprise of our life when we pulled into

Shaniko and saw the big crowd that was there (several thousand people) and we got another surprise when we saw that Shaniko ball team in action. They looked more like a Coast League team. The pitcher and catcher were from San Francisco. Wasco realized that they were outclassed, and going into the 4th inning, with the score 2 to 5 against them, a Wasco man tried to steal third base, and when he was called out, the whole team ran on the field and refused to play any more if that umpire wasn't fired."

"Most of the crowd was for Shaniko, and refused to change umpires. After arguing about two hours the Wasco crowd tried to split the bets up, but the rest of the people refused to do that, too, so most of the money went to the county. That was the wildest ball game I ever saw: Wasco refusing to finish the game, so many fights among the fans, so much money changing hands, and that wild ride back down to Grass Valley, Moro and Wasco.

"I hope some of those old timers who saw this famous baseball game are still alive, and remember when Shaniko was in her glory.

8

EARLY BUSINESS PEOPLE

William Reinhart

William Reinhart operated one of the early saloons in Shaniko and kept a rooming house before he became manager of Hotel Shaniko.

Reinhart was born in Germany and came to the United States with his mother and stepfather when a child. He left home as a young man to work in the coal mines of Ohio. When he learned he was suffering from the dread "black-lung" disease which had killed his father back in Germany, he decided to see as much of the world as possible while he was able. He hopped a freight train going west and landed in Oregon. The only work he could find was herding sheep. He met John Silvertooth and the two young men worked around the country on ranches or doing anything they could find to do. They finally managed to get into the saloon and hotel business in Shaniko.

In 1907, Reinhart bought 158 acres of land from The Dalles Land Office. When the Reinhart family left Shaniko in 1911 and moved to The Dalles, he sold the land to the father of Joe Morelli of Shaniko.

A.C. Sanford

A.C. Sanford was Pacific States Telephone and Telegraph Company representative in 1901, and was in charge of telephone rental, probably housing the telephone office in his store, or in a small building attached to it. He was City Road Supervisor in 1902.

William Reinhart and his wife Daisy Bell. Reinhart operated one of the early saloons and kept a rooming house before becoming manager of Hotel Shaniko.

At the Reinhart saloon on a warm evening, a group of men congregate to discuss the events of the day.

J.H. Coe

J.H. Coe, one-time partner of J.W. Fisher, was a council-man in 1902. Later he worked in the bank. City Council Proceedings reveal some details of his activities: "J.W. Coe, secretary of the Shaniko Band Concert & Amusement Company, requested a $500 loan from the City funds, stating the Band would give the City a mortgage on the lot and hall as security." It was not specified the lot and hall in question, but it may have been on "The Owl Roost," since the band practiced there.

The Coes had one daughter, Isabell. Mr. Coe was employed at Pease & Mays Company store.

D.A. "Del" Howell

D.A. Howell was chosen to fill the unexpired term of C.V. Palmer as councilman in 1906. Previous to that he had done road work for the city and was marshal in 1901. He was again elected to council in 1909. Convicted of murdering Mayor J.C. Fowlie in 1911, he served several years in the Oregon Penitentiary. He did not serve the full time of his commitment—it is said because his family moved to Salem to be near him and his good behavior shortened the term. It is not known where the family moved after his release.

John C. Fowlie

John "Jack" Fowlie came to Shaniko to manage the Eastern Oregon Bank. He first appears in city affairs in December 1904, when he was elected to the City Council. He became city treasurer, a post he held until he took office as mayor, January 6, 1909. In 1911, Mayor Fowlie was shot by the one-time marshal of the town, Del Howell.

There are several accounts of Fowlie's murder, but the one generally accepted is that Del Howell was brandishing a gun on the street near the bank when the mayor stepped up

Left: Mayor and Mrs. Dorothea Fowley. Mayor Fowley was shot on the street in front of the bank in Shaniko - the only known murder to take place in the town. *Right:* Mrs. Dorothea Fowley and her small daughter Lois moved to Rufus, Oregon, after her husband's death, where Mrs. Fowley's brothers owned the Fleck Orchard.

Stirring the mulligan stew after the rabbit hunt in Thorn Hollow: 1912 or 13.

to him and said, "Del, you'd better go home to bed, you're drunk." Hearing this, Del raised his gun and shot him.

After her husband's death, Dorothea Fowlie and her small daughter, Lois, moved to Rufus, Oregon. Dorothea's brothers owned the "Fleck" orchard, which furnished fresh fruit for much of northern Sherman County. Mrs. Fowlie lived there the rest of her life, and her daughter, Lois Fowlie Steward, still makes Rufus her home.

This is the only known murder that took place in Shaniko. There were wild threats, some shootings, a few knifings— mostly taking place in saloons or card rooms—but no other murders.

Life of the Women and Children

While the businessmen were tending their affairs, the women were not idle. Along with hours of household chores, they found time to put on box socials, programs, and chicken dinners to raise money for repairs to the fire-damaged community hall or some other project.

One occasion was recorded in the social news. The account described Mrs. Warren Wilson's Sewing Social. Each lady was given a pound of rags to sew in strips. The person to sew the most strips together in a given time received a prize. The strips were to be woven into the popular rag rugs of the day, a source of warmth in the winter cold. Wives of the most influential men in the community attended. No mention is made of the person who eventually received the finished product.

Children found many adventures around town, much the same as those described by Harry Hill. The city covered thirty blocks, but the hills and canyons just out of town beckoned the adventuresome. Any day spent in the canyons hunting, or just looking for a new discovery, was an adventure.

Sunday School Picnic, about 1912. *Top row, left to right:* Leola Loring, Mrs. Donley holding son Gordon, Mrs. Gus Reeder holding Ralph, Nora Widener, or Mrs. Peterkin, Mrs. Lucas and child, Mrs. Hoech and Irma, Louise Altermatt, Leslie Payne's mother, Mrs. Feldman (?), Agnes Schmidt, Lucille Schmidt, Bob Altermatt, Mildred Overman, Selma Johnson (teacher), (?), (?). *Next row, right to left:* Lenore Esping, Ferris Stocker, (?) Mrs. Alta Plaster Johnson and son Glea, Mrs. Plaster, (?), Elma Reeder, Elsie Reeder, F.T. Esping, Ina Page, Mary Overman, Dorothy Rosenbaum, (?), Donna Rosenbaum, Mabel Payne. *Front row from left to right:* Kenneth Payne, Arthur Schmidt, (?), Helen Overman, (?), Beula Esping, Madge Donley, (?), (?), (?), Gerald Johnson, (?), (?).

The small Rees children adventured around the large yard in their new Studebaker wagon.

A good place for such fun was a pond just north of town, which froze over in the winter. School children brought their skates and spent the noon hour on the pond. One time they pretended not to hear the school bell ringing to call them back to class—but a dutiful student chose to go back to the school, of course revealing the fact that the sound of the bell really was audible from the pond. Everyone else had to remain after school.

9

BRANDS AND RUSTLERS

Seasonal Work

Around Shaniko the farmers' busy season revolved around spring planting, summer harvest, and wheat and hay storage. While this work was being done, everyone worked long hours in the summer heat.

The sheepmen began an early season with lambing in April, shearing of the sheep in May, and the trek to summer range in June or July, and finally, the return in the fall to the home pastures. Extra workers followed these seasons as they progressed on ranches and farms.

The stockmen did not have quite the same work periods, although some ranches raised both grains and stock. Since horses and cattle from numerous ranches grazed together, unattended, in the canyons and on the bunch-grass-covered hills, it was important that the animals be marked or branded, if possible, before they were weaned. As soon as a colt or calf grazed away from the mother, it was difficult to determine its origin.

When a time for round-up was determined, cowboys from all the ranches drove the animals out of the canyons to their home ranch in a general "drive." Each outfit branded at home, then turned its stock back to the range separately. The brands used were easily recognized by stockmen, since each outfit evolved a brand of its own.

Oregon's Recorded Marks and Brands

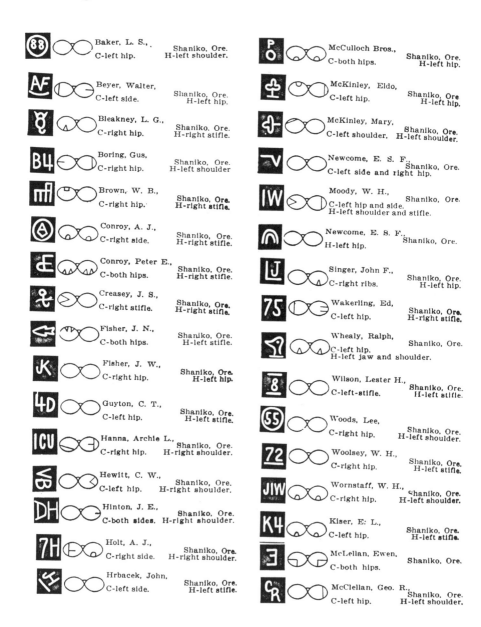

Baker, L. S.,
C-left hip.
Shaniko, Ore.
H-left shoulder.

Beyer, Walter,
C-left side.
Shaniko, Ore.
H-left hip.

Bleakney, L. G.,
C-right hip.
Shaniko, Ore.
H-right stifle.

Boring, Gus,
C-right hip.
Shaniko, Ore.
H-left shoulder

Brown, W. B.,
C-right hip.
Shaniko, Ore.
H-right stifle.

Conroy, A. J.,
C-right side.
Shaniko, Ore.
H-right stifle.

Conroy, Peter E.,
C-both hips.
Shaniko, Ore.
H-right stifle.

Creasey, J. S.,
C-right stifle.
Shaniko, Ore.
H-right stifle.

Fisher, J. N.,
C-both hips.
Shaniko, Ore.
H-left stifle.

Fisher, J. W.,
C-right hip.
Shaniko, Ore.
H-left hip.

Guyton, C. T.,
C-left hip.
Shaniko, Ore.
H-left stifle.

Hanna, Archie L.,
C-right hip.
Shaniko, Ore.
H-right shoulder.

Hewitt, C. W.,
C-left hip.
Shaniko, Ore.
H-right shoulder.

Hinton, J. E.,
C-both sides.
Shaniko, Ore.
H-right shoulder.

Holt, A. J.,
C-right side.
Shaniko, Ore.
H-right shoulder.

Hrbacek, John,
C-left side.
Shaniko, Ore.
H-left stifle.

McCulloch Bros.,
C-both hips.
Shaniko, Ore.
H-left hip.

McKinley, Eldo,
C-left hip.
Shaniko, Ore
H-left hip.

McKinley, Mary,
C-left shoulder.
Shaniko, Ore.
H-left shoulder.

Newcome, E. S. F.,
C-left side and right hip.
Shaniko, Ore.

Moody, W. H.,
C-left hip and side.
H-left shoulder and stifle.
Shaniko, Ore.

Newcome, E. S. F.,
H-left hip.
Shaniko, Ore.

Singer, John F.,
C-right ribs.
Shaniko, Ore.
H-left hip.

Wakerling, Ed,
C-left hip.
Shaniko, Ore.
H-right stifle.

Whealy, Ralph,
C-left hip.
H-left jaw and shoulder.
Shaniko, Ore.

Wilson, Lester H.,
C-left-stifle.
Shaniko, Ore.
H-left stifle.

Woods, Lee,
C-right hip.
Shaniko, Ore.
H-left shoulder.

Woolsey, W. H.,
C-right hip.
Shaniko, Ore.
H-left stifle.

Wornstaff, W. H.,
C-right hip.
Shaniko, Ore.
H-left shoulder.

Kiser, E. L.,
C-left hip.
Shaniko, Ore.
H-left stifle.

McLellan, Ewen,
C-both hips.
Shaniko, Ore.

McClellan, Geo. R.,
C-left hip.
Shaniko, Ore.
H-left shoulder.

The 1917 Legislature, seeking to make valid the use of marks and brands as legal evidence of ownership, passed a law making it illegal (a crime) for any person to brand or cause to be branded, any horse, gelding, mare, mule, ass, jenny, foal, bull, steer, cow, heifer, or calf without first having such brand recorded as required by law. The person fulfilling the requirement of registering a chosen brand and paying $1 had the exclusive right to use that brand for an indefinite period of time or until ownership changed. The transfer of a brand to the ownership of another person was a legal transaction which had to be witnessed by two other persons. The tool with which the brand was made was not to be confused with the brand as it appeared on the animal itself, including earmarks or other flesh marks recorded in conjunction with the brand.

Various earmarks were commonly included in the marking of stock. The owner of brands and markings specified where they were to appear on cattle ("C") or horses ("H")—mules included. Thus, the brand of Walter Beyer of Shaniko is:

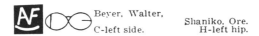

Beyer, Walter, C-left side.   Shaniko, Ore. H-left hip.

The brand on his cattle is seen to be found on the left side, and on horses, on the left hip. The earmarks shown in the double oval, describe slits as seen from the front of the animal. Horses were not ear branded. In recent years, a tattoo is placed inside the ear of horses and show cattle, so the mark does not deface the animal.

Rustlers

Rustling was not uncommon on the hills around Shaniko. Since much of the bunch-grass land had remained unplowed, horses, cattle, and sheep grazed on "home land" of farmers who often owned hundreds of acres of uncultivated range. In 1915 or 1916, the communities of Criterion, Bakeoven, and Shaniko were abuzz with the word that C.E. Matthews of Criterion was bringing charges against Ewen McLennan, a "prominent stockman of Shaniko," and Malcolm McDonald, McLennan's employee, charging them with stealing and later killing two horses.

The Dalles Chronicle
May 27, 1915 (or 1916)

"The Dalles, Ore. Ewan McLennan, a prominent stockman of Shaniko was found guilty on a charge of larceny of two geldings. . ."The case involves the stealing and killing of two horses belonging to C.E. Matthews of Criterion. The evidence introduced by the State showed that the horses were seen near McLennan's ranch in August with his brand on them. In November the horses were seen in McLennan's pasture with other horses belonging to the defendant.

"Matthews went to McLennan's ranch November 27 to look for his horses. Not finding them, he went through McLennan's pasture and found the carcasses of the horses with their heads cut off and the brands peeled.

"Matthews and five other men, including Gus Reeder, deputy sheriff of Shaniko, searched the whole canyon in which the carcasses were, unable to find either the heads of the horses or the brands.

"The defense of McLennan's was that the branding and killing of the horses on his ranch was a "plant" by his enemies. Matthews and McLennan, according to the evidence brought out in the case, have had an ill feeling for each other for the past ten or eleven years."

The jury deliberated 17 hours before finding MeLennan guilty and Malcolm McDonald not guilty. This was not an isolated case, as may be inferred from the roundup account of W.C. Guyton. Often the owners were either reluctant to go to court or unable to secure sufficient evidence of theft.

Another interesting case of theft was reported in the same newspaper under Bakeoven heading about the same time (1915 or 1916):

"Frank Fleming, on going to his barn Friday morning found his saddle horse and riding outfit gone. He started the Ford and tracked the horse to Shaniko, where all trace was lost.

"The man who had taken the outfit wore hob-nailed shoes. Mr. Mays arriving at Fleming's about noon, told of a man at his place the night before hunting work, and he noticed he was wearing hob-nailed shoes.

"That afternoon when Mr. Fleming was going home he overtook a man walking and asked him to ride. Then when they drove to the barn and the man got out, Jess noticed his hob-nailed shoes, and Mr. Mays identified him as the man who was at his house. They asked the man who gave his name as George Battie, where the horse and outfit were and he said he would show them where it was hidden. They found the horse tied in some thick brush at Thorn Hollow. Battie said he was coming back to the ranch to get another horse, as he didn't like the one he had taken."

10

A RIVAL RAILROAD

Shaniko—Fifth City in Size

Although the youngest town in age—incorporated in 1901—in a short time Shaniko became Greater Wasco County's fifth city in size and its first community in volume of business. This exciting progress continued for ten years. Ten years of shipping millions of pounds of wool each year. Ten years of loading out carloads of grain. Ten years of prosperity for hotels, stores, livery stables, saloons and many small businesses.

During this early period thousands of people passed through Shaniko: lived and worked there, or came in to file on land claims and homesteads. The townspeople had grown accustomed to the sounds of bleating sheep or bawling cattle waiting in the stockyards to be loaded on the train. The creaking of freight wagons laden with clumsy, mammoth sacks of wool was as familiar as the whistle of the train down at the road-crossing near the trestle north of town. In those first ten years, the sounds of construction, hammer and saw, were seldom missing.

The Rival Rail Line

In 1909, the railroad magnates Edward H. Harriman and James J. Hill, both got the idea of building rail lines up the Deschutes River Canyon from the Columbia River, south. Being determined men, neither would yield when he learned of the plans of the other, so the race was on, to see who could finish the rail line first. For months, workmen labored on both sides of the canyon building trestles and roadbeds.

The work was done almost entirely by men with teams and hand scrapers, picks and shovels. There was heated rivalry among the workers, even some sabotage of each other's supplies. The futility of this rivalry became apparent, and eventually an agreement was reached between the two companies who built their roads to Madras. However, from a point called South Junction, only one track was in use. Eventually, the railroad connected with lines reaching California. The road on the east side of the river was abandoned. Some of the old trestles can still be seen on the east wall of the Deschutes gorge.

Construction materials and the workmen reached Shaniko by train and were hauled by wagons the 20 or more miles to work camps in the Deschutes Canyon. Shaniko boomed with this influx of men and materials. The transient population filled saloons and gambling tables. The wide-open activites prevailed once more, until the City Council took measures to curb lawlessness. Additional police details were authorized. Long lists of levied fines appear in the Municipal Court records during 1910-1911.

The workmen moved on south and, as they went, other little communities began to develop. When the rail line was completed in 1911, the trains began their long runs south and these small communities drew business which formerly had gone to the rail terminal at Shaniko.

The metropolitan community of Shaniko became just another small town at the end of a branch railroad line. Shaniko and the Columbia Southern Railroad Company no longer handled business from great distances. Local farmers and stockmen were still coming to town to ship their wool and wheat, sheep and cattle. They were still in need of lumber, fuel, hardware and groceries; but Shaniko had been cut off from future growth.

The year 1911 was a fateful one for the City of Shaniko. The same year which saw the rival railroad drain away her life blood saw fire sweep through the business district, destroying most of the buildings. They were never rebuilt.

The phenomenal growth of the City of Shaniko had spanned a brief ten years, 1901-1911. It would never again be the Wool Capital of the World, though much wool and wheat continued to be shipped out on the Columbia Southern Railroad line. Trainloads of sheep and cattle were still loaded from the stockyards. Actually, there were numerous reprieves for the City of Shaniko. It took many more years for the town to die.

11

WAR YEARS, 1916-1918

Citizens of Shaniko responded wholeheartedly to the liberty Loan Drives and the sewing project of the Red Cross Society. Following are some items from *The Maupin Times* during the year 1918:

"The Red Cross Society at Shaniko has made 148 pillow slips, 115 hand towels, 63 sheets and 23 pairs of pajamas. These articles were cut out in The Dalles under the direction of the Red Cross Society there. Six sweaters have been knit and others will be finished soon. Mrs. Altermatt was elected chairman and Mrs. Henton secretary. They meet every Wednesday and Thursday at the Red Cross rooms at the depot."

"The Junior Red Cross is making gun wipes and hospital bags. They have finished 61 bags."

"J.W. Hoech, local chairman of the Third Liberty Loan Drive, attended the county meeting in The Dalles Saturday night and is prepared to instruct his committee, W. Bolton and John McLennan of Antelope and William Rees and Thomas Gavin of Shaniko. The drive begins April 6 and continues for three weeks."

"A Third Liberty Loan rally was held at the school house Friday night. A patriotic program was rendered. J.W. Hoech announced that Shaniko's quota was $35,000.00, but $40,000.00 already had been subscribed."

"Red Cross workers here are piecing quilts. Shaniko is expected to donate 100 pounds of clothing for the war stricken women and children of Belgium and northern France."

"The masquerade dance here Saturday night was well attended. People came from Antelope, Kent, Bakeoven and Grass Valley. The prizes were awarded to Mrs. Nelson, dressed as a Red Cross nurse and George McLellan as a sailor. The French's Jazz Orchestra from Grass Valley furnished the music. Supper was served at midnight."

"Shaniko is a claimant for Liberty Loan laurels. Without wishing to underestimate the performance of the Town of Powers, which averaged subscription of $100 for each man, women and child, and was accorded highest rank in the United States, Shaniko calls attention to the fact that with less than 300 population it contributed $52,200 or $174 for each man, women and child."

Adelbert Rees sold the first $50 Liberty Bond in the State of Oregon to A.P. Jones of Shaniko. Mr. Jones worked for the Union Pacific Railroad as a section man.

The Influenza Epidemic of 1918

Those who lived through the "flu" or Spanish influenza epidemic of 1918 will not soon forget the fear that gripped each community as their loved ones came down with the disease. The epidemic broke out in France in 1917, causing many deaths as it swept across the western world. Soldiers returning home at the close of World War I brought the Spanish influenza with them.

There was no known cure for the disease. Doctors treated their patients by whatever method appeared effective. It was still common practice for doctors to be called to the home of critically ill patients. Dr. M.D. Taylor drove his rig from Grass Valley to the Rees home on his weekly visit to the sick in Shaniko and Antelope. There he learned of especially severe cases and made his rounds where he was most urgently needed. He finally hired a driver so he could snatch a little sleep on the long drive. On one trip he said he had not had his clothes off for over a week, day or night.

Sometimes a whole family became ill at once. Any family with one well member considered themselves lucky, for that person could care for the rest. There were recurring epidemics of the disease for years, but they were less and less severe.

The war and the "flu" epidemics were over, but as people returned to normal living, a new epidemic broke out— bootlegging.

Moonshine and Bootlegging

In 1919, Congress passed the 18th Amendment to the Constitution, forbidding the manufacture, sale, and transportation of intoxicating liquors in the United States and all its territories. The Volstead Act providing for enforcement of this Amendment was passed January 16, 1920. This was to change the pattern of business for everyone connected with saloons and the way of living for those who consumed alcoholic beverages in and around Shaniko.

Some of the saloonkeepers moved away and found other occupations; a few removed the barroom trappings and converted to soft drinks, or set up pool halls. In some instances the change was only skin deep. For those who really wanted a drink, one could usually be found.

Bootleggers were busy outside the dance halls, but there seldom was any drinking seen by dancers.

Shaniko was considered an outpost in the interior, as far as county and state law enforcement was concerned, but raids were sometimes made by the county sheriff or Gus Reeder, his deputy in Shaniko.

Bootleg whiskey - sometimes the finished product left the consumer physically ill (or dead). It often made men violent. Mary McKinley's sketch tells the story as she saw it.

The proprietor of a saloon in a nearby town opined, "The United States may go dry, but our town will never go dry," and he continued to sell liquor across the bar in his accustomed manner, except when the sheriff from The Dalles made a raid. Then, for a few hours, the town was dry.

Rum running became a game in the populous cities near the coast, but inland, considerable trade was supplied by stills on the lonely hillsides where roads did not carry regular traffic. A tent would be pitched near some creek, miles from anywhere. In it would be a kerosene stove, a still, and the grain necessary to brew the whiskey—soon called "moonshine" (probably so-called because the still was tended mostly under cover of darkness). Sometimes the finished product left the consumer physically ill (or dead). It often made men violent.

There were no safeguards against contamination. Little sanitation could be practiced in the handling of beverage and containers. Gallon jugs were commonly used, but so were bottles of nearly every kind, even fruit jars.

A laughable story concerning the law enforcement efforts of the Shaniko marshal went like this;

"On a dark night, one of the well-known bootleggers had just made a sale outside a dance hall. Unbeknownst to him, the marshal had just come around the corner of the building when the bootlegger reached in his back pocket to get his flask holding the drink. The bootlegger's surprised voice was heard to say, 'I don't know what Gus Reeder's hand is doing in my pocket, but here is is.' That invalidated the sale; alcohol and flask were confiscated then and there."

Bootleggers, being innovative people, found many ways to camouflage their stills. One of the stories concerns a raid undertaken by Levi Chrisman, Wasco County marshal, who went out to a ranch where turkeys were being raised. The rancher expressed surprise that anyone would think he would be bootlegging. The thoroughness of Mr. Chrisman was not to be diverted. Before he left, he had located the still under a turkey roost.

One man had a still covered by hay in the barn. To get to the barn it was necessary to walk through a corral in which a wild and dangerous horse was kept.

Dangers were involved which affected the bootleggers themselves. It was not a good idea to horn into someone else's territory. This was serious business. There were rumors of feuding among the local entrepreneurs. Arson was an accusation not infrequently heard.

Prohibition brought benefits seldom recognized now, or remembered. Many law-abiding families put drinking away. They saw no liquor advertisements or displays in grocery stores. It was a beautiful time of hope and relief for some, a time of frustrated thirst for others. Then, during the first term of Franklin Roosevelt, the 18th Amendment was repealed (1933), and so the effort Herbert Hoover referred to as "The Noble Experiment" came to an end.

12

THE 1920's TO 1950's

Warehousing in the 1920's

In the 1920's a small crew still loaded and unloaded wood, coal, wheat, and other commodities completely by hand. Should a carload of coal be shunted onto the siding, the warehouse crew was soon at work shoveling coal into the deep wheelbarrows—which would hold up to a half ton—wheeling them over a coal pit on a 16-inch plank, then dumping the contents into the pit several feet below. One slip would have catapulted worker, wheelbarrow, and coal into the pit. Or, if a carload of slabwood arrived, it was unloaded piece by piece and piled to be sawed later. The wind was a factor at this elevation, blowing barkdust into the eyes and up coat sleeves of the workers. A man knew his physical strength and endurance while employed in warehouse work.

Sheep Shearing in the 1920's

The use of hand shears for shearing sheep was discontinued by 1920 when power-operated clippers came into use. Their power was from a "jack-shaft" which ran the length of the shearing barn. This shaft was driven by a one-cylinder engine with big, heavy flywheels to keep the power constant.

A good shearer could shear a sheep in about two minutes just to show his skill, but he averaged considerably more time than that. The work must have been back-breaking as the shearer wrestled each sheep to the floor. All the shearing was done in a stooped positon.

Sawing wood. *Left to right:* Harry Rees, Frank Wagner, Bill Kramer, Adelbert Rees. Wood came in carload lots and was unloaded by hand, then stacked for the saw; a gasoline powered motor was used. On windy days the bark splinters from slab-wood blew up the sleeves and down the necks of the workers.

After shearing, each fleece was tied with paper twine and the fleece was rolled into a neat ball before tying. The fleeces were then tossed up to the sacker who had a burlap sack about six feet high suspended on a ring inside a framework. This was constructed so the sacker could get down inside the sack and "tromp" the fleeces down. These sacks would weigh about 400 pounds.

The wool was baled at the warehouse in the early days, unless hauled to market by truck.

Sheep Herders

The men who herded the vast flocks of sheep for Hinton, Fisher, and others out on the "Flat" between Shaniko and Madras, or Maupin, spent most of their time in the field or range with the sheep. Supplies were brought by the camp tender, who was often the only person the herders saw for weeks at a time. The sheep dogs were indispensable and constant companions, relieving the tedium of dawn-to-dark watch over the sheep. The dogs knew as well as their masters

By the 1920's power-driven shears quickly removed the fleeces and a good shearer could finish a sheep in two minutes - to show his skill - but the average time was considerably more than that.

Power from a jack shaft driven by a gasoline engine made the work faster and easier for the shearers.

Left: The shearing began as soon as the animal was wrestled to the floor, the work done in a stooped position; it was tiring work. Notice the paper strings hanging from the shearer's belt. As soon as a fleece was ready it was rolled and tied with string and thrown up to a man whose job it was to sack the wool. *Right:* The six-foot burlap sack was fastened to a high frame. After the sack was a third full, the sacker "tromped the fleeces down" so the sack would hold more wool. The weight of a full sack averaged 400 pounds.

Moving the bulky sacks to position in the warehouse took several men - and sometimes a faithful dog to oversee his master's activities.

how to keep the flock together, seldom requiring more than a gesture of command. When a herder had a few days off (or got paid), he headed for Shaniko and one of the saloons, or to the Pastime for a game of cards. (Gambling was a sporadic event during the 1920's to 1940's; dependent on who came to town). When he had had enough of the "good life," the herder headed for the ranch and another three to six months with the sheep and his dog.

Not all herders were men. Occasionally a woman spent time with the sheep. Mary McKinley grew up in the sheep business. Her father, Henry Wakerlig, and her uncle, Solomon Hauser, were among the early "sheep kings" in the Bakeoven area, and she helped her father herd sheep as early as 1882.

There is a story concerning Charley Belshee of Sherman County who wanted 500 head of sheep taken 19 miles to the John Day Breaks, about 1927. The route lay through the wheat fields. The problem was to keep the sheep from trampling down the wheat. The regular herders said, "It can't be done," but Mary McKinley took on the job, which paid $3 a day. She moved the 500 sheep without disturbing the grain and without the help of a sheep dog.

At that time Mary McKinley had raised five children and knew the discomfort of working in heat, snow, and bitterly cold wind. She could wield the sheep shears as good as any man; she said, "I can do anything a man can do."

Stockyards

The Moody Warehouse Company owned the stockyards and furnished personnel to load livestock on the railroad cars. Ranchers brought cows and calves into the stockyard, separated them there, and shipped out the calves. Cows would return to the yards looking for their calves, and set up a clamor, bawling night and day, before finally giving up.

Not all herders were men. Mary McKinley grew up in the sheep business. She helped her father Henry Wakerlig and her uncle Solomon Hauser herd sheep as early as 1882. There is a story concerning Charley Belshee of Sherman County who wanted 500 head of sheep taken 19 miles to the John Day Breaks through the wheat fields. The regular herders said, "It can't be done," but Mary McKinley took the job which paid $3 a day. She moved the 500 sheep without disturbing the grain and without the help of a sheep dog.

When sheep were brought in to load, a "lead sheep" was a great asset. Sheep are quite stupid and contrary and it took patience to teach one to respond to a lead rope. A huge wether named "Bill' was used as a "Judas goat" to get the sheep to follow up the loading chutes. When he entered the car he was snubbed up close to the door so he could get out easily when the deck was loaded. The sheep were then usually shipped in double-deck cars.

The stockyards were dismantled after the railroad tracks were taken up in 1943.

Farmer's Elevator

In the early years of World War I (1916-1918) a group of farmers around Shaniko contracted with Hedges & Hull Company of The Dalles to build a warehouse and elevator

In the early years of World War I (1916-1918) a group of farmers around Shaniko contracted with Hedges & Hull Company of The Dalles to build a warehouse and elevator in Shaniko. When the warehouse and elevator were full of grain it was necessary to pile sacks in the yard. Fortunately the dry climate preserved the wheat in good condition until it could be shipped to market.

in Shaniko. The early managers were Cole Smith and Lew Alden. Charles Werner followed them, until a broken arm made it necessary for him to take a leave of absence. Tommy Jones took his place until Werner returned from Portland, where he had attended Behnke-Walker Business College.

The warehousing scene was changing. Formerly all wheat had been stored in gunnysacks, sewed in the wheat fields, and hauled by wagon to store in neat piles, 25 sacks high, with a corridor down the center and aisles to reach the wheat of different owners. By the 1920's, however, wagons had largely been replaced by trucks. Bulk handling of wheat moved by machinery and stored in bins was a great saving of labor. Elevators were being built throughout the wheat country.

Frank Wagner, who had been employed by Moody Warehouse Company since 1910, bought the Farmer's Elevator Company around 1940. In 1942, Bill Rees sold him the Rees Warehouses (formerly owned by Moody.).

Still more changes were to come. Farmers began hauling their own wheat and sometimes sheep or cattle to The Dalles or Portland, to market. The Columbia Southern Railroad (long since bought out by Union Pacific) began to be a liability rather than a big-paying enterprise. The company began scheduling intermittent service.

Guano—By-Product of Sheep Raising

On ranches around Shaniko, the lambing sheds were built with a roof high enough that a man on horseback could ride into the shed. In these sheds the ewes gave birth to their lambs in the cold spring weather and the lambs were sheltered until strong enough to go to pasture. If the weather was bad later in the year during shearing, the sheds were again in use.

About 1930, sheep guano had filled these sheds until a grown sheep could barely stand in them. Stockmen were glad to have this accumulation of manure removed. Truck gardeners in the Willamette Valley were eager to build up their soil, so the guano was in demand. The Dutcher brothers living west of the mountains, had their own trucks with which they could haul commodities back and forth from the Portland area to Shaniko. Joe Dutcher and his son-in-law, Reuben Ader, and Frank Dutcher and his sons, Merwin and Dick Dutcher, began transporting the fertilizer first in trucks, then by train. They found it was a paying proposition to haul cedar posts to the warehouses and ranchers of Shaniko, and return loaded with sacked sheep guano. It was not easy or pleasant work but it paid well enough.

Some of the crusty manure was shipped as bulk fertilizer by rail. It was ground on the farms, shoveled onto the trucks, then loaded into box cars. To fill the cars to capacity it was necessary to move the material to the back of the cars with a slip scraper, pulled by a mule from outside the car.

This was a thriving business until the accumulated supply of guano was exhausted—probably five years.

A Short Reprieve

The location of Shaniko was in the city's favor, since it was built at the crossroads of travel between the Columbia River and Klamath Falls, going north-south, and The Dalles and Canyon City, west-east. The flow of traffic changed with the end of the gold mining at Canyon City. Where the heavy road use had been between the eastern part of the state and The Dalles, the main flow of traffic became north-south. The road system of Oregon was slowly evolving from the primitive dirt roads of horse-and-buggy days to graded, graveled surfaces.

Pete Olsen was foreman of a crew that worked on the dirt roads before gravel was used. (Pete's son Ivan owned and operated Gavin-Wheeler Company store in later years.) A four-wheeled grader pulled by a caterpillar tractor was used to remove ruts and throw out rocks in the spring after the roads dried out.

A north-south highway was built by the State of Oregon in the 1920's. At first it was called "The Dalles-California Highway", designated as a "military road" in 1925. This road bore no resemblance to the Military Road of the 1860's. Extensive planning was done to make it a direct, fast highway, one of the best in the West. It is now known as "U.S. Highway 97," the fastest road from California to Washington. Truck and car traffic is heavy.

The building of Highway 97 and the grading and improving of secondary roads in southern Wasco County was a three-decade undertaking which furnished a reprieve for the dwindling community of Shaniko. For 30 years Shaniko periodically headquartered the crews of workmen and often their families, all of which brought business into town, keeping alive the earliest tradition of a transient population.

The network of county roads, particularly the steep grades into the Antelope and Clarno canyons, took years to build and, later, to improve. State and county road departments maintained the roads between Clarno, Antelope, Shaniko, and to the Sherman County line on #97 north, as well as west to a junction with The Dalles-California Highway (U.S. 197) from The Dalles, on south.

At intervals the school population would increase and sometimes be doubled by families who lived for six months to two years in the community. The tent houses of the beginning of the century were duplicated by their counterparts, camp cabins, which had little to offer in comfort, being constructed much the same as homestead cabins had been. The Shaniko Hotel also housed visitors.

Some of the earliest live-in trailers were seen in Shaniko. Usually very small by today's standards, they allowed little more than room for a walkway between rooms, but were at least a home with some semblance of permanence.

Decade of 1920

By the late twenties there were accepted social patterns in Shaniko. The business people making their living there were likely to socialize mostly with each other. They included Mrs. Moody, Frank Wagner, Mr. Gavin and the Wheeler, Hoech, Rees, Kinney, Altermatt, Reeder, and Rhodes families. The social events of these permanent residents were much like those of their counterparts in The Dalles or larger towns. Without intent to be exclusive, they often entertained each other at dinners and afternoon and evening bridge parties. Special food and sometimes flowers were delivered from The Dalles by train for an occasion. Sterling silver and snowy damask linens appeared on their tables and their homes were made festive for the occasion.

Families not engaged in a permanent business often came and went, just as work was available. When times were hard they returned to Shaniko because rent was cheap, or they owned houses, and there was a chance they might get work on one of the ranches. No one was really "stuck" in Shaniko. Generations of Shaniko families persisted in this coming and going. The return was a "home-ing."

What social life many of these people engaged in was different from that of the business community. They were likely to entertain out-of-town company or relatives, to seek diversion individually. Some chose not to engage in community affairs. They did whatever they chose. A few drank the weekends away with friends. Seldom did these activities come under scrutiny.

The Great Depression of 1929

There was little warning of the coming depression of 1929. After the stock market crashed, shock waves crossed the country, never stopping until they had reached the smallest towns in Eastern Oregon. Shaniko was no exception. Bank runs were feared so much that Eastern Oregon Bank closed its doors. They were never opened again. Everyone connected with the bank moved away. (It was one of the few banks in the state that paid the depositors 100 cents on the dollar.)

The one-time Pease & Mays Store, long since owned jointly by Thomas Gavin and Roy Wheeler under the name of Gavin-Wheeler Company, felt the loss of business so severely that Roy Wheeler sold out to Gavin and left for Washington. The only businesses that survived, aside from the gasoline stations, were the Rees Warehouse, Farmer's Elevator, the store, hotel, Gus Reeder's Harness Shop and the Pastime.

Hitchhiking became a way of life for teen-agers and adults as they traveled from California to Washington looking for work in harvest. Since Shaniko was at the crossroads, the town saw many distressed people, let off from one ride and waiting for another. (It is 35 miles south and 17 miles north to the first shelter and water.) Sometimes a couple with small children would stand on the turn of the highway most of a day waiting for a ride.

Ranchers were offering $30 a month wages—if they were hiring. Several families who had been gone from Shaniko for years returned and managed somehow to get along. Almost everyone learned how much they could get along without. People helped each other as they shared garden produce. Sometimes the city furnished out-of-work people with fuel during severe weather.

This depression was to break some of the ranchers and stockmen of Central Oregon, who had borrowed from the banks as long as their credit was good, then asked the merchants and warehousemen to extend credit as long as they could. W.A. Rees had been extending credit to many of these men. He knew from them how they sweated it out with the bank before they finally signed for loans they might not be able to repay. He described the situation in a poem written in 1930:

The Hard Times of 1930
By the Bard of the Sage Brush

The sheepmen of Old Oregon are the very best of men—
They still carry checkbooks and a pencil or a pen.
Most of them are cheerful and say they're feeling fine
When they step into the sweatbox and sign on dotted line.

There's Anderson and Johnson and Peterson, all Swedes.
A-riding round the country checking up on sheepmen's needs.
I suppose they know their business, but it almost makes one weep
When you hear a Swede tell a Scotchman how to run a band of sheep.

Hoot Mon, and there's the Scotchmen, they deserve a lot of praise,
The McDonalds and McLennans, the McPhersons and MacRaes—
They take a drink of whiskey, they do not care for wine
When they walk into the sweatbox to sign on dotted line.

The Irishmen are good stockmen and they are also smart—
They always have the cash to buy a gallon, pint or quart.
They smile at the depression but the poor Scotchman wilts
When he's lost his life-time gathering and has to don the kilts.

They curse the stores and warehouses and say that times are hard
And rave about the prices of bacon, beans and lard.
But one time when they're happy and you'll never hear them whine
Is when they're in the sweatbox signing on the line.

They give their bank security and are told that's not enough,
And the banker acts as if he'd weep when he says, "Have you more stuff?"
So they dig up more security and the banker says, "That's fine!"
When they leave the sweatbox and have signed on dotted line.

The Dutch sheep man works very hard to get out of the kinks
And when you ask him how times are, he says, "Ain't this the Yinks?"
You talk to another sheepman and I'll tell you it's no joke
When he points his thumb above his head and says "Why, hell, I'm broke!"

Wasco County became so strapped for money that land in small towns including Shaniko was sold for taxes at public auction.

The depression gradually edged the town nearer oblivion. Even with the Civilian Conservation Corps providing work for a number of young men, there seemed little future for the community.

In general, Shaniko people probably suffered less than those in cities. The number of people out of work was not so overwhelming.

World War II

About the time that people were getting their second wind, the United States entered World War II. What few young men there were left in Shaniko were soon drafted. A number of families moved away to get work in the shipyards. Unemployment became a thing of the past. But there were now not enough children in town to maintain a school. By 1944, the six or so children of grade-school age were sent to Antelope to school and the two or three high-school students went to Moro for their classes. (Later, all students were bussed to Maupin.)

Similar changes were taking place in the community around Shaniko. There were few small farmers or ranchers left. Most of the land had been incorporated into large ranching operations, Bakeoven being a good example.

The Hinton-Ward Ranch

In 1932, when jobs were hard to come by, George Ward went to work for Jim Hinton at the going wage of $25 a month and room and board, doing farm work. The job soon paid $35, which may have established the permanence of the relationship between Hinton and Ward. When Ward married Mary Hampton of The Dalles, it was understood he would have a permanent job with Hinton. The young couple lived on the Hinton ranch near Bakeoven.

Five years later, Hinton sold a partnership interest in his—by then—65,000-acre holdings to George Ward; and the Imperial Stock Ranch built up by R.R. Hinton became known as the Hinton-Ward Ranch. On retiring, Hinton sold out to Ward.

At one time George Ward had a total of 15,000 head of sheep in summer bands, in addition to 3,000 yearlings and ewes with lambs. At the conclusion of feeding on summer range, the young sheep were shipped to market directly from Sisters, Bend, La Pine, and Crescent. In the spring they were shipped by train to the mountains out of Maupin and South Junction.

During the time he ran large bands of sheep, George Ward leased land on the Warm Springs Indian Reservation, called "Mutton Mountain." Some sheep were pastured on Crane Prairie Forest Service land.

After Hinton sold his holdings, George Ward bought even more land. When the grass was short, he leased private land from logging companies. But the era of vast herds of sheep grazing on bunch-grass-covered hills was nearing its end. Synthetic fibres began to take the vast market so long enjoyed by wool. Ranchers found that with prosperity returning, it was difficult if not impossible to keep enough herders with the sheep. The lure to work in the city at better wages made it unlikely that young men would ever take the place of the old herders dying off. Sheepmen then turned to the raising of cattle, in great demand as meat consumption rose.

So the Ward operation began running beef cattle more than sheep. It was possible to pasture cattle year-round on lands Ward owned. He began producing grass-fed steers, usually turned off to market when three years old. One rider was with the stock all the time while on the range. When they were being shipped to or from the range, the cowboys would load their horses on a trailer and drive the truck to meet the cattle at their destination. So the sheep country gradually changed to cattle country and the means of transportation changed from trains to trucks. Large trucks hauled not only grains and wool, but transported stock from rural communities, bypassing the railroad.

End of the Shaniko Trains

Shaniko Line was no longer the most productive run in the Northwest. The daily run was cut to three trains a week, then two, and finally, the train arrived only when a carload lot was ready for shipment. Regular passenger trains had not been on the line for years when, in 1941, the company recorded the transport of eight passengers in the whole year and those had ridden on the freight trains.

The Union Pacific Railroad Company, by this time owner of the Shaniko branch, petitioned to close the line. The I.C.C. determined that the volume of wheat to be moved warranted maintaining bi-weekly service at least as far as Kent. In July of 1943, permission was given to take up the rails from Shaniko to Kent. The next step was to end service between Grass Valley and Kent, leaving rails only as far as Grass Valley.

End of the Columbia Southern Line

Weather finally settled the fate of the Columbia Southern Line. In December 1964, an unusually heavy snow fell, followed within a few days by strong chinook winds. The snow melted rapidly. Then it began to rain. Throughout Central Oregon the water rose in creeks and rivers, overflowing their banks and washing out bridges and roadways. There were about ten days when communications were cut between numerous towns. Bill Hanks and other citizens with CB radios relayed messages from stranded motorists to their families at home.

By the time the flood waters reached Hay Canyon in Sherman County, they had become a raging river. Railroad tracks and, in many places, the very roadbed were washed away. In Biggs Canyon the rails lay twisted and scattered.

When the waters subsided and the inspection of damage was completed, it was apparent that the roadbed could not be replaced, and the Shaniko Line was no more. However, times were changing, and had it not been for the flood, the branch railroad would have been closed anyway within a few years. It was June 20, 1967 when the legal closing took place.

Trucks Take Over

When the larger trucks began lumbering through Shaniko at increasing miles per hour, the sharp turn in front of the hotel became hazardous. The State Highway Department responded to complaints by sending a crew to design an alternate and broader curve to be located behind the hotel. C.C. Seeley was in charge when the work began, and Forrest Cooper was the locating engineer. John Hess and Jimmy Don were draftsmen. This curve, built with an experimental technique, took many months to complete, often isolating one part of town briefly from the other. First the roadbed was graded down deep and sprinkled until muddy; then the mud was mixed with oil and allowed to set. Gravel was added and eventually the whole was surfaced. It must have been well done as the curve has remained in good shape all the years since. Forrest Cooper went on to become the state highway engineer in Salem (since retired).

Later Days at the Shaniko Hotel

In the 1940's occasional guests were still registering for the night at the Shaniko Hotel, when the owner, John McLennan, retired from raising sheep in the Antelope country and moved into the hotel to live. At that time, to an outsider, life in Shaniko was pretty much "Ho-hum."

One afternoon two strangers came into the hotel lobby and registered for the night. In the morning they were gone—and so was Johnny McLennan. The staff and people living in the hotel were mystified about Johnny taking off without his breakfast and leaving no message. Days went by and there was no word from Johnny. When the townspeople learned of his disappearance, they became alarmed. Concern about his safety prompted someone to send for his brother, Duncan, who was living in Montana. There was no evidence of foul play, so aside from reporting him as a missing person, there didn't appear to be anything that could be done.

About three weeks went by before Johnny returned as abruptly as he had left. He appeared very nervous and distraught. He said only that he had been kidnapped and forced to write checks. Beyond that he would only say, "I wouldna' tell any mon about it." He died about a year later, never having recovered from the experience. His brother Duncan remained in Shaniko and operated the hotel.

Duncan was a generous man with a fine Scotch burr and a joy in living. He was soon bringing the old stockmen out on the "breaks" of the canyons to the hotel to live, when they

were too sick or too old to remain on their small holdings—
and he took care of them till they died.

Things Looked Up in the 50's

In the 50's, things were looking up for the Shaniko community. A state highway maintenance garage was built and a work crew lived in town. The great telephone system reached the vicinity and surveyors and workmen were headquartered there. Following that was the building of the huge gas pipe line from California to Washington. Again workmen lived in Shaniko.

When these crews left, it was not long before the state highway maintenance garage was closed and the several families moved away.

The handful of people left by that time had been around long enough not to quarrel with their environment or the rise and fall of the number of residents. They didn't mind the "isolation" or lack of physical refinements. They were a pretty self-sufficient lot with no thought of asking anyone's help just because of the town's loss of population.

There were still two and sometimes three service stations pumping gas and selling road supplies, one of which, Pat & Bill's, housed the Shaniko Post Office.

Joe and Sue Morelli

Joe and Sue Morelli leased the Shaniko Hotel from Duncan McLennan in 1952. It seemed a good place for them; Joe's health was poor but he could tend the lobby and do chores. Sue was a registered nurse who soon saw the possibility of using the vacant hotel rooms to house county ward residents. It was an excellent care facility for the ambulatory people who came there to stay. Sue was qualified to oversee health care, and the residents could safely wander around town or find small chores to keep them busy and happy. In 1954 Morellis bought the Shaniko Hotel.

13

GHOST TOWN

The year 1959 brought what was, perhaps, the last reprieve for the City of Shaniko. The State of Oregon was celebrating its Centennial Year at the Exposition Center in Portland. Featured in the displays were large bulletin boards with blown-up scenes photographed in Shaniko and captioned, "Oregon's Ghost Town of the Year." This was the first time Shaniko had been referred to as a ghost town. Visitors and camera buffs soon converged on the old town, even though that designation was premature.

The town had surely slowed down. Perhaps 40 people were in residence at the time. Gasoline and road supplies were dispensed at the several service stations. Children from town were taking the school bus to Maupin all week. The city government was functioning and the hotel was thriving with the influx of county wards.

There were residents who resented the conclusive tone used to describe their home town as dead. That feeling grew even stronger when curiosity-seekers invaded town, poking into unoccupied homes and, in several instances carrying away belongings from the houses. One indignant resident took his hunting rifle and stood in the street, refusing to let cars enter the lane leading to unoccupied private homes.

This period was brief. When it was learned that the Shaniko Hotel served home-cooked meals and displayed pioneer memorabilia on the walls of the dining room, the curious gathered there to learn more about the old town. Soon there were postcards to buy and brochures of Shaniko lore to carry home.

Joe Morelli beside the hardwood bar in the dining room of Shaniko Hotel. The Morelli's collection of elk heads, lanterns, and pioneer memorabilia filled the counters and walls. When people learned that the Shaniko Hotel served home-cooked meals and displayed memorabilia of the era, the curious gathered there to learn more of the town.

The Morelli's collection of elk heads, lanterns and pioneer memorabilia outgrew the counters and walls in the dining room, so they opened up the area formerly occupied by the bank. Their museum included pump organs, phonographs, hand-painted pictures and quilts.

Joe loved horse-drawn wagons—in fact, any form of early transportation. He built a wagon yard across the street from the hotel, where he eventually gathered together one of the finest collections of wagons, buggies, stage coaches, and other horse-drawn equipment in the Northwest.

The elderly residents at the hotel became an important part of the hotel crew. Visitors remembered Henry the "cop" or Howard the "sheriff." It was make-believe, but they became an addition to the Shaniko experience. People came from all parts of the Northwest and beyond. Photographers found the water tower, school house, and city jail interesting camera fodder. Weekdays, as well as weekends, brought visitors to see Oregon's most popular ghost town. Since no charge was made for visiting the museum site, donation boxes were visible in various buildings.

Joe Morelli loved wagons. He built a wagon yard and in time filled it with one of the finest collections of horse-drawn vehicles in the Northwest.

"Howard the Sheriff." The elderly residents of the hotel became an important part of the hotel crew. Visitors remembered Howard and "Henry the Cop." It was make-believe, but they became part of the Shaniko experience.

Lobby of the Shaniko Hotel, June 19, 1960. The old circular seat which was installed in the hotel in 1901 was re-upholstered after the Morellis bought the place. (Oregon Historical Society picture)

The increase in population put a strain on the water supply. Old wooden pipes and leaky joints in the city mains, made it impossible to maintain the abundance of water that had been enjoyed in the early days. The Morellis had a well dug. For about ten years it produced enough water before the flow diminished.

Ed Martin's Museum and Antiques

In 1961, Ed Martin bought the Pastime and a few lots in Shaniko from Joe Morelli and took some of his antiques there for storage. During 1962, Martin was a very busy man running the stage coach at the "Little World's Fair" in Damascus, Oregon. After the fair was over, he began to make serious plans for a museum in Shaniko. In 1963, he moved the rest of his antiques from Portland to the Pastime and other buildings he had acquired in the vicinity of the Shaniko Hotel.

Martin said he believed one of the cars he moved to Shaniko had been owned by Will Rogers—a 1923 Stutz. He showed a "puddle-jumper," a one-of-a-kind car, hand-built in 1924, and a stagecoach built that same year for the filming of the movie, "Bend in the River." After the railroad went through the Siskiyou Mountains into California, a last historic run was made by seven stagecoaches. One of the coaches was in Martin's display.

Property owners and people interested in promoting the Ghost Town of Shaniko and preserving its historic buildings, formed a club in the 1960's. In 1962-3, thirty people were considered members. They did the work repairing the city hall, school house, and some sections of the old sidewalk.

Ed moved the old Bakeoven school building to Shaniko. Joe Morelli, Ed Martin and Wayne Harris restored the city hall and jail. Although Joe was unable to contribute physically, he furnished shingles, lumber, etc., for restoration projects, while Ed and Wayne contributed their labors.

Weekdays as well as weekends brought newcomers to see Oregon's most popular ghost town. Families came with their children to eat the family-style meals served at the hotel. Youngsters loved to climb over the wagons, investigate the old jail, and thrill at railroading tales of the past, or sit in the caboose across the street.

Shaniko was becoming well known again. A sequence of the television show, "Moving On" was made in town, starring Claude Akins and Frank Converse.

About 1970 the Morellis bought the Shaniko Warehouse from Blue Line. It had stood vacant since Commodity Credit Corporation was phased out by the government, and the wheat surplus became a part of the past.

Joe's health grew worse. He was up in his wheelchair during the day but was in much pain. Nevertheless, he enjoyed visiting with people who came to the hotel. In June of 1971 he died. After Joe's death, Sue encountered problems with the Wasco County Health Department concerning fire pro-

Ed Martin bought the Pastime and some other buildings from Morelli and moved his collection of antiques to Shaniko. He worked with others to repair the jail, city hall and sidewalks. Martin moved the Bakeoven schoolhouse to Shaniko and brought in a caboose which he put alongside the museum. The false western fronts on the buildings were also his work.

Ed Martin built a new post office in 1972 when Shaniko was a busy ghost town. Designed to harmonize with architecture of the turn of the century, the post office is the newest building in town. The postmaster sells postcards, stamps, and gift items to the daily visitors.

Senator Mark Hatfield visited Shaniko.

The TV series "Movin' On" used Shaniko as a setting for one of the shows to be shown in November of 1974. Claude Akens shown with Sue Morelli.

tection and sewage disposal. She was told that the water supply could not furnish adequate fire protection and the old method of draining sewage over the brow of the hill would not be permitted if the hotel was to house county wards and serve meals to the public.

As mayor, Sue made every effort to get grants for the city's water and sewage systems. Governor Tom McCall and Senator Mark Hatfield helped to get together possible grants which were later tabled and then outdated.

Since Sue could not comply with the health and safety codes of the county, she was forced to sell the Shaniko Hotel, its furnishings, the antique memorabilia, and the wagon yard at auction (October 14, 1977). "It was a sad day when the Shaniko Hotel was a victim of the auctioneer's gavel and the old hardwood bar and mirror from the earliest furnishings were hauled away to Salem. Other antiques found their homes all over the Northwest," said Sue.

With the closing of the hotel, Martin then also closed down his historic displays. He continued to operate the new Shaniko Post Office which he had built late in the summer of 1972.

After Sue left, the scattered residents hoped to be able to keep the ghost town image alive. They applied for Federal grants to repair the schoolhouse and keep the hotel functioning as a tourist accommodation. A small sum of money was received, so with volunteer help, repairs were made to the schoolhouse.

In 1980, application was made to the National Register of Historic Places to have certain pieces of property in Shaniko designated as a Historic District. The map indicates this comprised the area from Third and Fifth Streets, bounded by "D" on the west, to the Columbia Southern Railroad site on the east. In addition, the water tower, school and old Wilson home were included.

14

SHANIKO TODAY

The town of Shaniko may be reached from the Columbia River Highway by taking route 97 south through the wheat-lands of Sherman County. In the spring the fields of green wheat contrast with the brown summer fallow to form rectangular patterns as far as the eye can see. By harvest season the rolling hills are a beautiful golden russet. Sherman County contains some of the most productive wheat fields in the United States.

After passing the town of Kent, the road leaves the wheat fields, crosses the county line in Wasco County and begins a steeper climb over the hills. There terrain changes. The soil is rocky with bunches of grass and yellow sage never touched by the plow. This is grazing land. Soon the road climbs and winds up out of Kelsey Canyon and emerges over the brow of the hill—where there is more bunch grass and sagebrush.

Then Shaniko appears, its once familiar silhouette now changed. The round grain elevators are gone—blasted down in 2001. They were the first concrete grain towers in Wasco County, once rising above one of the largest wool warehouses built at the turn of the last century, now owned by Robert B. Pamplin, Jr.

Still standing on the western boundary of the city, like a huge cracker box on a pedestal, sits the old water tower. Efforts are underway to save this historic structure from the wrecking ball.

As the highway nears town, off to the left, the old rail-road bed is gradually wearing away with the passage of time and changes in weather.

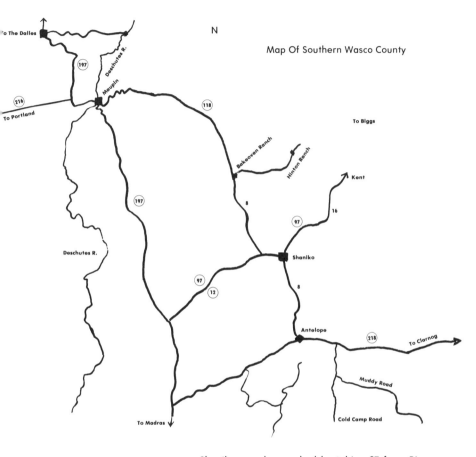

N

Map Of Southern Wasco County

Shaniko may be reached by taking 97 from Biggs Junction south through Sherman County, directly to Shaniko. From Portland the route would be to take highway 26 east. Change to 216 at a junction on the mountain. Just before reaching Maupin, follow 197 through Maupin and over the hills to a junction with 97 which is located 12 miles west of Shaniko. Continue on 97 to the town.

The schoolhouse bell tower is one of the first sights as you approach Shaniko.

The unique outline of the school building catches the eye before the city limits are passed. Its central bell tower forms a peak above the roofline. The Shaniko School opened in 1901 and operated until 1944, and then again for grade school in 1950-51. The Farrell family headed efforts in 1989 to further restore the school Help was received in the form of a grant from the Fred Meyer Trust in 1994. By the following year the building was opened for community use. The first Shaniko School Reunion took place in July 1997, and the second in July of 2000. Both were attended by many alumni and their families.

Passing the "Entering Shaniko, Population 25, Drive Carefully" sign, the highway enters Shaniko on "E" Street. The current population of Shaniko is uncertain. As throughout its history, the population of Shaniko fluctuates, with few residents who have lived there for more than twenty years.

At the first intersection an old building displays a new sign, "Yankee Trader" along with the old "General Store" sign which has hung there for many years. This building was the original "Owl Roost" of Shaniko's earliest days.

Highway 97 makes a broad curve to the right here, leaving "E" Street and cutting behind a large brick hotel. In less than two minutes the through traffic will have speeded west on 4th Street and will be out of Shaniko, headed toward the towns of Maupin or Madras, each approximately thirty-five miles distant. When the highway was first built, it continued straight on "E" Street another block and made a sharp right turn in front of the Shaniko Hotel. Increasing traffic and speed made this a dangerous turn, so the State Highway Department constructed a long, broad turn to make a safer road through town.

Where the highway turns, tourists continue on "E" Street a block to the intersection with 4th. This is the central area of interest. The old city hall on the left stands next to the tall, steel-framed bell tower, just as it has been since it was built in 1901. In this quaint two-story structure housed the city's water pressure tank on the first floor. Alongside the building runs a walkway giving entry to three barred cell doors. Early occupants of the three jail cells dubbed them "Snake-Pit", "Bum-lodging" and "Palace-sleeper". These small, bare cubicles were used to house suspects until they were taken to The Dalles by the county police, or as a place to detain drunks until they sobered up.

For many years a stairway from the street led to the council chamber above. In addition to the business transacted in the name of the City of Shaniko in this room, it was the place where the city recorder wrote: "There being no further business than to swat the wasps, the council meeting was adjourned, we donned our hats, and went home." (When a fire was built in the seldom used building, the wasps emerged in great numbers.) Money donated by several individuals along with money raised by the Chamber of Commerce, established in 1994, helped resident volunteers to put a new roof on the old City Hall in 1998.

The Yankee Trader is now in business in the General Store building, originally the "Owl Roost."

Highway 97 makes a curve to the right, leaving "E" Street. Tourists continue on "E" Street one block to the center of Shaniko.

The old City Hall and Jail sit on the opposite side of the tall steel-framed bell tower from the new City Hall, which opened for its first meeting in 1999. The new City Hall is only one of the buildings which Ed Martin (below) has moved to Shaniko and renovated for use by local residents and businesses.

Also in 1998, a small house was moved to the opposite side of the bell tower from the southeast edge of town by Ed Martin and others to serve as Shaniko's new City Hall. It opened for the first meeting in March 1999. The adjacent building bears the sign "Pioneer Saloon—Julius J. Wiley" and over the door "Tickets" is a tribute to Shaniko's early days when the first coaches, wagons and trains came to Shaniko. This building now houses the city's new water pressure tank. Across the street, the Shaniko Hotel covers half the block on the west side of "E" Street. Surprisingly, it appears about the same outwardly as it did when Frederick Shilling and his bricklayers slapped the last trowel of mortar on the frame and raised the porch over the front door. New possibilities opened up with the installation of the new water system for the town in 1985. Closed since the auction in 1977, the Shaniko Hotel along with other property in town was purchased by Jean and Dorothy Farrell. Restored to its former glory from rooftop to boardwalk, and now on the National Register of Historic Places, the Shaniko Hotel opened for business as a bed and breakfast in the fall of 1987. The hotel building also houses a restaurant, a gift and antique shop. The Farrell's displayed much of Shaniko's history in photographs and information in the hall-ways of the hotel, including an eye-arresting photograph of a large steam locomotive plowing through deep snow drifts. It is a reminder of the trains that brought the city to life in this lonely rangeland over one hundred years ago. This picture is one that was enlarged from a photograph taken by a Moro pho-tographer named Raymond, in the snowy winter of 1902, and enlarged by Hi Donley, an engineer on the Shaniko line, as an anniversary gift to his wife. Their son, Gordon Donley, and daughter, Madge Brown, presented the picture to the City of Shaniko at the dedication of the new Post Office where it hung for many years. In July 2000, Jean and Dorothy Farrell sold the hotel along with the Shaniko Corral RV Park, Ice Cream Parlor and other property to Pamplin, who also purchased the

Popular with tourists in the hot summer sun, the Ice Cream Parlor was opened by Jean and Dorothy Farrell in 1997. The building, adjacent to the shady park with picnic tables, also currently houses an antique mall.

wool warehouse, grain elevators and almost thirty city lots from Lillian (Gastman) Hale.

The hotel dominates the central ghost-town area since it faces both on "E" and 4th streets with the front floor in the corner of the building.

On the south side of the hotel, facing, are the buildings which had housed Ed Martin's museum. Period storefronts were attached to the old buildings during its early ghost town days. Today the buildings house shops catering to tourists offering antiques, gifts, jewelry and more. At the west end of that stretch of buildings stands the Post office, built in 1972 by Ed Martin who designed it to harmonize with the architecture of the early 1900s. The thirty-five post office boxes are rented to both local and out-of-town residents.

Across from the Post Office, next to the hotel, sits a shady park next to the Ice Cream Parlor, popular with the tourists in the hot summers of Shaniko, and more retail stores.

Back down 4th Street, opposite the hotel to the east is the wagon yard built by Joe Morelli, displaying a collection of horse drawn equipment. Ed Martin's collection of antique cars is now housed in the old livery stables on the south side of 4th street next to The Shaniko Sage Museum, which shares some of Martin's collections. In June 1996, Debra Tabor Holbrook began publishing monthly editions of *The Shaniko Sage* offering readers information on local history, news and events. The offices of *The Shaniko Sage* are housed in the Shaniko Sage Saloon & Trading Post, one of the group of small buildings located in the alley behind the city hall.

Around the corner, "E" Street continues south. The Martin's caboose which once sat across from the Pastime is no longer there. At the end of the road is the Shaniko Corral RV park, opened by

The old Bakeoven Schoolhouse is now used as a wedding chapel.

The historic wool warehouse and round cement grain towers as they looked prior to 2001. The first concrete grain towers in Wasco County, they once rose above one of the largest wool warehouses built at the turn of the last century.

Jean Farrell in 1989. Providing tourists with an alternative to the hotel, the RV park offers spaces for RVs and tents.

A block away, the Bakeoven schoolhouse, moved to Shaniko in 1964, has been restored and now serves as a wedding chapel opened by Jim Hogan. His advertisements offered a "Western Wedding in the Historic Ghost Town of Shaniko." Since Hogan's death, Shirley Stevens now performs the weddings at the chapel.

At the east end of 4th, along the empty railroad beds, looms the great, elongated Shaniko Warehouse, which housed millions of pounds of wool in the first years of use. It sat empty for years, except for the period of time when Dave Gastman housed his collection of old warehouse equipment there. Pamplin, the current owner of the warehouse recently rennovated the structure, although additional modifications are needed before it can be used by the public, hopefully in the future it once again play a central part in community functions. The century old cement grain towers were brought down about the same time. The old Farmer's Warehouse is gone now too.

Located on the west side of town, at the cross roads is Ken's Place at Shaniko, offering groceries and gifts along with gas. At

Along with gasoline and other car related items, groceries and souveniors can be purchased at Ken's Place.

one time owned and operated as a Texaco Station by Leo Butcher and his wife, Ken and Pat Comstock are the current owners of the building which had originally been the old Post Office. It was moved to its current location by Bill and Pat Hanks who remodel it for use as a service station-post office after Ivan Olsen closed, then tore down, the old Pease & Mays store building which had be located on that corner.

County Road 218, south to Antelope, veers of "C" Street beside Ken's Place, and begins its descent into the deep depression of Cross Hollows, a half mile away. Three old springs, boxed in cement, are visible on the right in the cross-draw. The sturdy dual-cupola-crowed barn built by Leslie Payne still stands along with one other building amidst the ruins of other outbuildings. The house nearby was home to the Reeder family while Gus was city water-maintenance man.

On the right side of the road, faint tracks can be seen between where the house and barn once stood, leading up the hill a few yards to the place where Ward's Stage Station and blacksmith shop stood in 1874, and where the stage drivers exchanged exhausted horses for fresh teams. On the left of the road, a clearly visible dirt road leads down the cross-canyon to the Shaniko water works one-eighth mile below the barn. At one time there were two buildings at the reservoir. The taller of the two buildings housed the pump and pressure tank that lifted water to the City of Shaniko. A long, one-story flat structure was built to cover the reservoir, into which water runs from springs on the wall of the rapidly-deepening canyon.

The old Bakeoven route to Cross Hollows once entered what is now 6th by the Water Tower, then turned south and skirted the brow of the hills above the present road to reach Ward's Stage Station.

Considerable work needed to clean and repair the reservoir in the canyon, as well as restore the mains to the city on the hill, was financed in part by CETA, the Federal Government's Comprehensive Employment Training Act. After several starts and stops because of lack of funding, it wasn't until 1985 that the

The old Water Tower still stands, although it is in need of immediate repair. Note the Shaniko Fire Department truck in the foreground.

new water system went into operation. The pump is located at the reservoir but the old water works buildings have been removed.

Also under the CETA program, the original boardwalks in front of the city hall and along the post office block were repaired, and a vacant lot was leveled for a city park where picnic tables were shaded by small locust trees.

Today in Shaniko, the Chamber of Commerce is raising money for continued renovations of the town by selling "Old Shaniko: The Ghost Town" bottled water from the Shaniko Springs Bottled Water Company, supplied by Byron Jacobs who shares his time between Vancouver and Shaniko.

The town of Shaniko plays host to hundreds of tourists each year. Because the town is so visible on the heavily traveled high-

Western re-enactments are popular with the hundreds of visitors who come to celebrate Pioneer Days or the Shaniko Festival every summer.

way people continue to stop in Shaniko. Drivers, noticing the "Ghost Town" signs, pull off highway 97 to see what is there. Buying postcards, ice cream and souvenirs, they wander the streets of town, admiring the collection of wagons and cars, speculating on the use of the three jail cells in the old city hall before getting back into their cars and resuming their journey.

Some people plan a trip to Shaniko because they once lived there, or have seen or heard about "the most popular ghost town in Oregon" and they want to share what they have seen or heard with someone else. A number of them wander around with metal detectors, or recount to their children or their companions the memories they have of a former visit, incident, or event they know or have read about the wool-capital heydays. Many come to join

On the" Journey Through Time" route, Shaniko holds a special place on the maps and in the memories of many who pass through the "liviest ghost town in Oregon" every year.

These small buildings in the alley behind the city hall house the office of *The Shaniko Sage* and Miss Lucy's Boudoir Botique. Plans are being made to house more of Shaniko's history in the other buildings.

in the Shaniko Festival, or the Pioneer Days which bring visitors from far and wide to witness the reenactments, dance to the bands and take in the historical displays all over the town. Shaniko has also become a favorite destination of motorcycle clubs looking for a great place to stay at the end of a long, interesting ride; history buffs following the "Journey thru Time" route from Biggs to Baker City; and those looking just to get a glimpse of the way life used to be.

As highway 97 leaves Shaniko headed west, the bunchgrass, rock scabs, and sagebrush stretch for miles in all directions, all ringed about with purple hill. Once the city limits have been passed, the same unchanged plateau of the 1890s appears—as though over a century of time has stood still. Except for the roadway and an occasional fence or homestead cabin, it is the same as when the first explorer gazed across the "flat."

The future of Shaniko in this seemingly unchanging land is once again in question. Ed Martin, Wayne Harris, Jean and Dorothy Farrell, Joe and Sue Morelli and others like them in the past, have contributed much time, effort and financial backing to make Shaniko into the liveliest ghost-town in Oregon. Many of these people are now either gone or unable to participate much anymore. However, the lively ghosts of this village do not give up easily. Just as in any town, businesses open, close, or change hands. People move in and out. Residents, both full time and those who live there for the busy summer months, and others for whom Shaniko holds a special attraction, hold out hope that the future will honor the past and preserve Shaniko, its buildings, boardwalks, and all. Because of its history, because of its people, Shaniko continues to hold a special place in the history books, on the maps and in the memories of those who have come to know it.

SHANIKO CHRONOLOGY

1862—Canyon City Gold Rush, which brought about the establishment of the stagestop at Cross Hollows.

1872—Scherneckau built his first building at Cross Hollows. AT Cross Hollows.

1879—First Post Office at Scherneckau's stage-stop.

1887—Scherneckau sold the Cross Hollows business and moved to Astoria, Oregon.

1897—First recorded school at Bakeoven.

1899—Townsite Company formed.

1900—Federal Census showed a population of 172 in Shaniko (March 31).

1900—First construction train reached Shaniko, at that time a tent city (May 13).

1900—First passenger train reached Shaniko (June 1).

1900—The new Pease & Mays store building burned (October 2).

1900—1903—Two hotels, several livery stables and numerous homes erected.

1901—Lord & McLaughlin started to build Shaniko Warehouse (February).

1901—First regular meeting of Town Council of Shaniko was recorded (March 16). February 9, application for incorporation of city was filed.

1903—Shaniko became "Wool Capital of the World," shipped 2,229 tons of wool, 1,168,866 bushels of wheat, and held wool sales of $3,000,000.

1903—First severe smallpox epidemic.

1903—During the second of three wool sales, W. A. Rees deposited over a million dollars in the bank, one day's sales for Moody Warehouse Company.

1904—Estimated total amount of wool sold, $5,000,000.

1905—Sidewalks extended, making Shaniko a city with the best sidewalk system in Central Oregon.

1910—Population according to United States Census was 600.

1911—The Oregon Railroad & Navigation Company railway was completed up the Deschutes canyon and south, ending the era of phenomenal growth for the City of Shaniko. That year fire destroyed most of the business district.

1921—The first high school class graduation.

1925—The Dalles California Highway was completed, and trucks began taking local trade from the Columbia Southern Railroad Company and from the City of Shaniko.

1934—The last class graduation from Shaniko High School.

1936—Railroad passenger service ended.

1942—Regular freight service ended on the railroad. The tracks were removed from Shaniko to Kent.

1955—Joe and Sue Morelli bought Shaniko Hotel.

1959—Shaniko was first called a "Ghost Town" at the Oregon Centennial Exposition in Portland.

1964—Flood waters washed out the railroad bed and rails in Hay--Canyon, northern Sherman County, and Biggs Canyon.

1978—Shaniko Hotel was sold at auction (October 13).

1980—Application was made to the National Register of Historic Places to designate four areas of the city as a National Historic District.

1985—New water system goes into operation.

1985—Jean and Dorothy Farrell buy the Shaniko Hotel.

1986—Arthur Fine publishes *The Bitter Seed*, a fictional history of Shaniko.

1987—The Farrell family begin to renovate the Shaniko School.

1989—Shaniko Corral RV Park opens.

1994—Shaniko Chamber of Commerce established.

1994—School House restoration continues with a major boost from a Fred Meyer Trust grant and volunteer labor.

1995—One side of the School House opens for community use. Projects continue inside.

1996—*The Shaniko Sage* begins publication by Debra Tabor Holbrook (June).

1997—East rooms of the School House open with beginnings of schoolroom display.

1997—Shaniko School Reunion (July).

1997—Bakeoven School opens as a wedding chapel.

1997—New Ice Cream Parlor building opens.

1998—New City Hall moved next to the Old City Hall (July 7).

1998—New roof put on the Old City Hall by resident volunteer help with money donated by several individuals and the Chamber of Commerce.

1999—New City Hall opened for first meeting (March).

1999—Don Schmidt posts 27-page website, www.shaniko.com (April).

2000—Special fund account opened for official plans to save the water tower.

2000—Second Shaniko School Reunion (July).

2000—Robert B. Pamplin, Jr. puchases Shaniko Hotel, Grain Elevators, Wool Warehouse, Ice Cream Parlor Building, Shaniko RV Park and other property in Shaniko (July).

2001—Grain Elevators blasted down and Wool Warehouse rebuilt.

BIBLIOGRAPHY

Braly, David. *Tales from Oregon Outback.* America Media Co. 1978.

Brogan, Phil. *East of the Cascades.* Binford & Mort. 1964.

City of Shaniko Council Proceedings. 1901 - 1923.

Federal Census. 1900.

French, Giles. *The Golden Land.* Oregon Historical Society. 1958.

Guyton, Ada Bell. Unpublished Diary. 1897 - 1950.

Holst Publishing Co. *Progressive Reference Library,* Vol. 4.

Krier, Jean. *St. Paul's Episcopal Church Centennial Booklet.* Optomist Printers. 1975.

McKinley, Mary. Unpublished Diary.

McNeal, William Howard. *History of Wasco County,* self-pub., 1933.

McNeal, William Howard, *Old Wasco Country Pioneers,* self-pub., 1975.

Military Road, the. J. W. Allen, Introduction Lulu Crandall, The Dalles Historian.

Moody Warehouse Co. Records 1906 - 1909.

Oliver, Herman. *Gold & Cattle Country.* Binford & Mort. 1962.

Oregon Railroad History, Ida Engle.

Shaniko Born of Error. Myrtle Wagner. Oregon Journal.

Shaniko Leader. 1902 Issue.

Shaver, F. A., Adams, A. E. *Illustrated History of Central Oregon.* Western Historical Pub. Co. 1905.

Sheep Leave Mt. Hood. Sunday Oregonian, Oct. 12, 1930.

Thomas, Mrs. Bert C., Aulona Ch. DAR, Klamath Falls. *First Ladies of Oregon.* Klamath Falls *Herald & News.* 1960.

Turnbull, George S. *Governors of Oregon.* Binford & Mort. 1959.

VanDersal, Samuel. *State of Oregon Recorded Marks & Brands.* Kilham Stationery & Printing Co. 1918.

INDEX

D

Dairs, 25
Davenport, Homer, 42
Davis, Guy H., 61
Dethlefs, Otto, 24
Detjen, 22
Doering, Gertrude, 83
Don, James, 129
Donley, Mrs. and Gordon, 99, 146
Donley, Hi, 146
Donley, Madge, 99,146
Dorres, W., 40, 41
Dunlavey, George W., 61
Durbin, Charley, 9, 11
Dutcher Bros. Joe, Frank, Merwin,
   Dick, and Reuben Ader, 121

E

Eagle Hotel, 44
Eastern Oregon Banking Co., 41, 56,
   61,124
Eastkraut, Antonia, 70
Elrod, J. O., 40
Esping, Al, 78
Esping, Beula, 99
Esping, Frederick T., 99
Esping, Lenore, 99
Estabennet, "Frenchy," 42
Estabennet, Katy, 73

F

Farmer's Elevator Co., 120, 124
Farr, 5, 69
Farrell, Jean and Dorothy, 146, 147, 149,
   156; Family, 142
Feldman, Mrs. E. F., 99
Fisher, J. W., 96, 115
Fisk, Frank, 82
Fitzpatrick, Mary Emma "Maria," 22
Flanagan, John, 54
Fleming, Frank, 104
Fleming, Jesse, 17
Fleming, Leo, 17

Fowlie, Dorothea, 97, 98
Fowlie, Lois, 97, 98
Fowlie, Mayor J. C., 60, 61, 62, 96, 97
Fred Meyer Trust, 142
French, D. M., 28
French, E. H. and V. H., 40
French, J. W., 29

G

Garrett, Maud, 68, 69
Gastman, Dave, 59, 62, 150
Gatsinger, Frank, 62
Gavin, Thomas, 44, 57, 59, 62, 67,
   68, 109, 123, 124
Gavin Wheeler Co., 67, 122, 124
Glade's Shell Station, 65
Glavey, Mike and Tom, 9
Gott, Edna, 82
Guyton, Claud T., 10
Guyton, Will C., 9, 104
Guyton, William F. "Dad," 11

H

Haight, Charles, 5
Hale, Lillian (Gastman), 147
Hall, Alma, 82
Hamilton, Lil, 90
Hampton, Mary, 127
Hanks, Mary Ada "Pat," 68, 69, 151
Hanks, William "Bill," 69, 129, 151
Hanna, Edith, 82
Hanna, Phyllis, 81
Harriman, Edward H., 106
Harris, D. J., 34
Harris homestead, 26
Harris, Wayne, 136, 156
Hatfield, Senator Mark, 138, 139
Hauser, Clara, 16, 18
Hauser, Conrad, 16, 18
Hauser, Rose, 16, 18
Hauser, Soloman, 16, 18, 20, 118
Hauser, Solomon (son), 16, 18
Hauser, Susette, 16, 18
Henry the "Cop," 133, 134

Helen Guyton Rees and her husband,
William Adelbert Rees

Helen Guyton Rees was born on a homestead near the station of Wilcox, near Kent, Oregon, March 30, 1910, of homesteader parents. Her grandfather, William P. Guyton, left Ohio in 1860, crossed the Isthmus of Panama and sailed to San Francisco. He prospected for gold in Nevada City, California, and at Idaho City, then part of Wasco County, Oregon. When the gold rush was over, he rented a wheat farm at McMinnville, Oregon, and settled down with his bride, Mary Ellen Smith.

The Smith family had worked its way west from Virginia, coming to Oregon from Iowa—"Crossing the Plains" in 1865. Ada Bell, the mother of Helen Guyton, was the granddaughter of John and Emily Bell, who also crossed the Isthmus of Panama, but in 1852.

Pioneering was in the blood of the family. Mrs. Rees has traced ancestors back to 1732, in Calvert County, Maryland, as well as in Virginia. A saying of both families is, "We've been around this country a long time." It is natural that Mrs. Rees would be observant of the customs and ways of the pioneer community of Shaniko. Firsthand experience permeates the book she has written.

Her life has included doing farm chores as a girl, attending at grade and high school at Kent, seventeen miles from Shaniko, then business college in Portland before her marriage to William Adelbert Rees of Shaniko. The couple lived in Shaniko for thirteen years. Early in World War II they moved to Fairview, Oregon, where she worked part-time for seventeen years as clerk for her postmaster husband. William Adelbert Rees died in 1992.

Their four children scattered to far places. The eldest, The Rev. Wm. R. Rees, and his family lived near Medford, Oregon, at Shady Cove. Richard, the second son, was a steel worker in Long Beach, California. Both sons past away in 1999. Anna Bell Rosene, the only daughter, is a retired elementary teacher who lives with her husband in Boring, Oregon. The youngest, Charles, lives with his wife Patricia in Columbia, Maryland, and teaches at the University of Maryland Law School in Baltimore.

Mrs. Rees is interested in Episcopal Church affairs and the Ecumenical Community in East Multnomah County. She enjoyed selling SERRV hand-crafted items imported by Church World Service to provide self-help for workers in underdeveloped countries. She has written three other books: *Schoolmarms*, *Shaniko People* and *Guytons Galore.* Now 91 years old, Mrs. Rees lives in Portland, Oregon.